CRICKET
TALES Un

Controversies and Contributions

Raju Mukherji

Notion Press

No.8, 3rd Cross Street
CIT Colony, Mylapore
Chennai, Tamil Nadu – 600004

First Published by Notion Press 2020
Copyright © Raju Mukherji 2020
All Rights Reserved.

ISBN 978-1-63633-785-2

Publication Profile

- First published through Amazon KDP in June 2020

- **KDP ISBN:** 9798651392490

- ©Seema Mukherji. Seema Mukherji has the moral right to be identified as the copyright holder of this work.

- All rights reserved. No part of this publication may be reproduced in any form without prior written permission from the copyright holder.

- **Publishing Consultant & Presenter/Editor:** Sachin Bajaj, Managing Director & Founder, *Global Cricket School**

- **Editorial Consultant:** Soma Banerjee

- **Chief Editor:** Arijit Mukherjee

- **Assistant Editors:** Sounak Das and Seema Mukherji

Dedication

A token of gratitude
to all my talented pupil-friends,
to all my meticulous and generous readers
and
to all other true connoisseurs of Indian Cricket

From the Presenter's Desk

Cricket India: Tales Untold, is my third book with Raju and I am pleased to present it to the readers.

Being associated as a patron and administrator of cricket for many years, involved sharing the same boat with many servants of the game across the country and globe – some not to be spoken about and some to be highly spoken about – their ethics, commitment, humility, integrity, intent...

This book personifies all the virtues spoken above. It uncovers the facts which were hidden till now, unravels the general understanding and fearlessly palates the unpalatable truths from the history of Indian Cricket.

Such an effort was necessary for the sake of the game and the true connoisseurs of Indian Cricket.

With this, I hope that the cricket loving fraternity comes to know a bit more than the conventional history of the game in India and how it achieved its current status.

– Sachin Bajaj
Managing Director & Founder,
Global Cricket School
www.globalcricketschool.com

Contents

Acknowledgement

This book is the role model of all team efforts! No individual in this team of 'FAB FIVE' can be pinpointed for special credit. Everyone contributed handsomely. As the eldest in the team, I am exercising my discretion to say a few words more than the others.

My young pupil-friends — Sounak Das and Arijit Mukherjee — both 30 years junior to me took the initiative to publish this manuscript that was gathering dust for quite a while. They volunteered, planned and acted so speedily that I was unable to offer them even a 'thank you'.

Seema   Soma   Sounak   Arijit

Foursome out of "FAB FIVE"

Arijit's wife and former journalist Soma Banerjee started the ball rolling. The brilliant lady's conception and invaluable guidance led us all the way towards the book's publication.

In just one week, Arijit edited the manuscript, selected the pictures, designed the cover and the layout as well as everything else to do with the publication. Absolutely outstanding.

Sounak was perpetually at hand with the arduous tasks of editing, correcting, co-ordinating and providing encouragement. Truly brilliant.

My wife Seema assisted profusely with the editing and endless cups of tea. Once asked, "West Indies is not one nation, but they play as one team. Why?" Thankfully was able to convince her that cricket takes pride in its anomalies!

Eminent lawyer Bishwajit Bhattacharyya loves cricket, loves me and is an outstanding writer himself. His wonderful Foreword is replete with compliments. Honestly, I quite enjoyed the praise in public.

For the Preface, I requested the young, 'cricket-nonconformist' lady of our team of 'FAB FIVE' to do the honours. Soma's delightful perception has convinced me that she has to write my obituary as well.

My thanks to all the newspapers and magazines where my articles appeared since mid-1970s. The list includes The Statesman, The Times of India, The Hindu, The Telegraph, Hindustan Times, Deccan Herald, Deccan Chronicle, Sportstar, Sportsweek, etcetera.

Rishi Valmiki did not write with readership, revenue and royalties in mind. As humble followers of the great sage, we too wish to follow his path. We can only say that those who read the text will get to know Indian cricket more intimately.

Raju Mukherji

Foreword

Bishwajit Bhattacharyya, Senior Advocate, Supreme Court of India & Former Additional Solicitor General of India

I first met Raju Mukherji in 1972 at Ferozeshah Kotla Ground in Delhi.

I was then 20 and Raju 22. As I was witnessing the match, one elegant square cut from Raju, off the back-foot, anguished the legendary bowler Bishen Singh Bedi, bowling from the Delhi Gate end. Bedi jumped and lifted his hands in despair, as the ball crossed the fence like a rocket. Perfect timing and an artistic shot! Raju supplied oxygen to East Zone, after a dramatic batting collapse. East Zone defeated the mighty North Zone in a very low-scoring tie. It was a Duleep Trophy match between Ambar Roy's and Bedi's respective teams.

Though Raju scored only 27 his class and character sparkled! My day was made when I managed to shake his hands, positioning myself near the Pavilion, and a smiling, suave Raju obliged an unknown fan with the warmth that has risen above time and above the norms of society!

Little did I realize then that we were to soon become batch-mates in a bank. I got to know more and more about Raju's sterling character, integrity and class. We remained in occasional touch throughout.

I was pleasantly surprised when I received a mail asking if I would write a Foreword to a book he proposed to publish about cricket. I was excited, but worried. What credentials do I have to write a Foreword on a book on cricket?

My cricketing ability pinnacled only when I carried drinks to Delhi University cricket ground, on interval, wearing full cricketing dress.

But then, I could muster the courage to write only after reading a portion of his manuscript.

What a classic book it is! I thought I must express that Raju's book reflects a carbon copy of the great human being that he is: straight, ethical, idealistic, committed, humility and integrity personified, yet unsparing to every wrong! Raju can never compromise with integrity and class!

Raju recounts how right from the inception of Test cricket in India, there have been selfless persons committed to cricket and to the nation. The appointment of "commoner" C.K. Nayudu as India's first-ever Test Captain in 1932 was not because of the selection committee, but because of magnanimous gestures of two princely gentlemen, Natwarsinhji and Ghanashyamsinhji, Maharajas of Porbandar and Limbdi respectively, writes Raju. These two Maharajas, appointed as Captain and Vice-Captain, sacrificed immortality for the just cause of the nation.

Raju portrays vividly the ups and downs of India's cricket administrators and players. Raju's praise about Rahul Dravid and Polly Umrigar has been touching. The book covers every stakeholder of Indian cricket: prominent cricketers, who have brought laurels and glory to India, as well as, the forgotten heroes, the immortal trio of Pavri, Baloo and Deodhar.

I congratulate Raju for his magnificent efforts. His painstaking research, piercing through hitherto unknown facts is amazing!

In closing, I am deeply humbled to be asked to write this Foreword. You will enjoy reading this book.

BISHWAJIT BHATTACHARYYA
Former Additional Solicitor
General of India

Preface

Soma Banerjee: A Knowledge Management Professional, Journalist, Literature Lover and *Anything But a Cricket Fan*

To say this is a book about cricket is a grave understatement.

With cricket at its soul, this book is a masterpiece of history – replete with accounts of rousing patriotism on one hand and petty self-centricity and malice on the other – the two opposing sentiments that make for the most intriguing study of human nature.

It is a tale of a young nation's grit to master the master's game and the legendary people who gave their all to lift not only the game but the country from subordination to equality.

Cover-drives, *line* and *length* here speak not just about technical excellence but of human spirit that rose above crushing social injustice and circumstantial evil to gift India some brilliant sportsmen.

Of an impoverished *harijan*, sweeping the cricket grounds in Pune, silently watching *sahibs* play from a distance, then going on to represent the Hindu team in the Triangular tournament in 1907– a story by itself in the caste-steeped early 20th century Indian society.

This book is also about the necessity to remember that the foundation of today's most lucrative game ever was laid by selfless maharajas who now don't find a mention even in the most avid cricket lover's kitty of anecdotes.

It is also about the enigma of human character. Of our country's most celebrated national cricket tournament, Ranji Trophy, being named after a man who vehemently stayed away from contributing to the Indian game. And being thus named by a man, an altruistic maharaja, who did everything to elevate the game but has been rarely acknowledged for it.

It recounts the contribution of an industrialist who offered a blank cheque to host the country's first world cricket championship, not because he loved the game, but simply because he loved his country.

Every page presents a burning desire to tell those untold tales only an avid worshipper and grateful son of the game can feel, and a masterful historian can execute.

"Raju Sir", as he is fondly called by his pupils, does just that – page after intriguing page – educating, informing, exploring, analysing.

"I want to be an academician first and only then a cricketer,' Raju Sir had once told his childhood idol, Dinkar Balwant Deodhar.

Raju Sir, Deodhar would have been proud.

– Soma Banerjee

Introduction

If you are not a former Test player, you are not eligible to be a current Test selector. Sounds quite logical. In fact, this notion has recently been made popular in our country. Actually, coming to think of it, if you are not good enough to play a Test match, you are obviously not fit to select players for the Test team. As simple as that.

Frankly by the same reasoning, people who have not played in Test matches, should not write or commentate on Test players as well. How will they be able to assess the worthiness of Test cricketers, when they themselves were not good enough to play Test cricket?

As with selectors, writers and commentators should also be barred from writing on Test players, if those writers and commentators have not played Test cricket. Let the logic be consistent for all, please.

I am not a Test player. Yet I have been writing and commentating on international cricket for nearly 50 years. The simple reason was the realization that post mortem on dead bodies was not done by dead doctors. The moment I realized that a judge need not be a criminal himself to judge a criminal, I decided that I would express my thoughts on Test cricket and Test cricketers by speech and in print.

Not being anybody's favourite has a distinct advantage. You do not have to fear or favour anybody. Or flatter anybody. You can relax and be your man. You can speak the truth without any hesitation. The power of truth will take you through. *Satya Meva Jayate*. God has blessed me in the sense that I do not owe any allegiance to any cricket player, media-house, administrator or sponsor.

This book is about the heroic deeds of those men which have been either erased from memory or purposely hidden from sight. These issues have hardly ever been raised.

The sole intention to relate these issues is to inform the discerning readers of the real image and heritage of Indian cricket.

This is actually a reverential homage to our cricketing forefathers and peers, each of whom sacrificed his self and soul for our betterment. Just to remind those heroic men, both in the Elysian Field as well as among us, that we have not forgotten their yeoman contribution to Indian cricket.

– Raju Mukherji

Nostalgia: Author In conversation with SMG

Princely States

Royalty at its Best: Patiala, Cooch Behar, Natore, Porbandar and Limbdi

House of Patiala

The House of Patiala has contributed immensely to the progress of cricket in India. In the 1880s when the Parsee community was promoting cricket in Bombay, the highly-ranked Maharaja of Patiala Rajendra Singh (1872 – 1900) began to encourage cricket in his dominion.

Maharaja Bhupendra Singh of Patiala

Later when his son Prince Bhupendra Singh (1892–1938) ascended the throne, the new Maharaja gave sports, particularly cricket, a new dimension in his State of Patiala. He was among the first of Indian princely families to appreciate the value of sports and gave encouragement to his subjects.

In 1911 Maharaja Bhupendra Singh organized and led the first-ever all-India cricket team to England. This team comprising players from all over the country – as against the exclusive Parsee teams of the 1880s – was the forerunner of all future India teams. In fact, this team was the first sports team to represent India in any sport.

Patiala's team was not restricted to any community or province. That would go completely against the grain of this generous visionary. The pioneering role of Maharaja Bhupendra Singh of promoting sport in India has been relegated to the footnotes. Really a shame.

Although the team did not do very well in terms of result – no one expected a group of first-timers to UK to do wonders – there is little doubt that the Indians displayed commendable technique and temperament to earn plaudits from the British media. This tour brought into forefront the undoubted genius of Palvankar Baloo (1875–1955).

Baloo, a *harijan* by birth, from Pune overcame social and financial problems to finally represent the Hindu team in the Triangular tournament, which began in 1907. His excellent control over spin and swerve made him the most dangerous bowler in the country. In England too, he maintained his form and was the outstanding success of the tour. The emergence of Baloo as a quality left arm spinner at the international arena would not have

Palvankar Baloo

been possible without the munificence of the House of Patiala.

In 1926 when Arthur Gilligan brought the MCC team to play matches in India, Maharaja Bhupendra Singh created an unusual record. He represented MCC against his own country! Those days whenever England went on tours, they would use the nomenclature MCC (Marylebone Cricket Club) instead of England.

As Maharaja Bhupendra Singh was a member of MCC, the MCC captain Gilligan invited him to play for MCC, in effect for England! The Maharaja played against India in India's first-ever unofficial Test at Bombay Gymkhana ground for MCC!

Bhupendra Singh also donated the Ranji Trophy, the symbol of inter-state supremacy in India's domestic first-class cricket. His son, the handsome Yadavendra Singh (1913–1974) was an exceptionally stylish batsman who stroked the ball with immense power.

The young yuvraj, Yadavendra, went one step ahead of his maharaj-father. While the father had played in an unofficial Test for MCC in 1926, Yadavendra Singh represented India in an official Test match in 1933–34. He played against Douglas Jardine's England (then MCC) at Chennai (then Madras).

Yadavendra, following his father's footsteps, represented MCC under Jardine against the Viceroy's team at Delhi in 1933–34.

On India's inaugural official Test tour of England in 1932, Yadavendra Singh was originally offered the captaincy. He declined to go as captain or player because of pressing State duties.

There is a mistaken notion that the first-ever 'royal personality' to represent India in official Test cricket was Iftikar Ali Khan, the senior Nawab of Pataudi. The credit goes to the impeccable credentials of the Yuvraj of Patiala, Yadavendra Singh.

Yuvraj Yadavendra Singh of Patiala

The tall, strong and handsome Sikh possessed a heart as big as his frame. Never took advantage of his royal status. Never craved for power. Knew not pettiness. In an age when 'royalty' was expected to lead on and off the field, Yadavendra Singh readily offered his services to play a Test match under the leadership of the 'commoner', CK Nayudu.

The opposition was England. The season was 1933–34 and the venue happened to be the first-ever Test at Chepauk in the heart of Chennai. With Douglas Jardine as the opposition skipper, no player – royalty or commoner – could expect any mercy.

The young prince of Patiala was an outstanding batsman, who smote the ball with immense power. Particularly fond of cover-driving, the ferocity of the hook stroke attracted him. To bat against the likes of Mohammed Nissar, among the fastest-ever, was no joke, especially on the coir-matting pitches of northern India. Yadavendra used the bat as a scimitar whenever he found the time for cricket from his busy schedule of Patiala State duties.

After the Tests at Bombay Gymkhana and Eden Gardens, where the Indian batting had not fared too well, the selectors opted for Yadavendra at Chepauk. In those days the Madras Cricket Club saw to it that the pitch had a rich layer of grass to make the contest between bat and ball even.

In the first innings, debutant Yadavendra Singh notched an uncharacteristic, sedate 24 to Vijay Merchant's 26. But in the second outing the young prince was at his attacking best against the likes of Headley Verity, Clark and Nichols. His ferocious hook to the left of the leg umpire had even the tough Jardine nod in approval. His magnificent 60 was India's highest score in the innings. The athleticism of Yuvraj Yadavendra came to the fore as snapped both the catches that came his way.

As it transpired, this Test was both his debut and swan-song. He was a certainty for India's following tour to England in 1936. But the Yuvraj could not find the time from his pressing duties as the monarch of Patiala. Cricket's loss was Patiala's gain.

The House of Patiala's contributions to Indian sports are too numerous to be mentioned here. Despite such magnanimous contributions to Indian cricket, neither father nor son ever jockeyed for posts in the hierarchy of Indian cricket. Ironically neither was ever a president of BCCI. They all along stayed away from its musty corridors.

They were among the wealthiest and the most influential of the royal families, yet they never bothered to dominate the BCCI. They helped Indian cricket like no other, yet they never stayed back to enjoy the benefits. They let the petty and the corrupt to crawl in the stench.

Patiala's contribution to Indian cricket has been forgotten because they never bothered about publicity or power. The great contribution of the House of Patiala should be written in words of platinum in the annals of Indian cricket.

House of Cooch Behar

The Maharaja of Cooch Behar, Nripendra Narayan Bhup Bahadur (1862–1911), was the foremost patron of cricket in Bengal in the 1890s, at about the time when the Maharaja of Patiala, Rajendra Singh, was vigorously promoting the game in north India.

Apart from providing fabulous cricket facilities both at Calcutta and at Cooch Behar in north Bengal, Maharaja Nripendra Narayan even brought over coaches from abroad to train the young Indians at cricket. His son Prince Hitendra Narayan played for Somerset in the English county championship in 1910. Nripendra Narayan's

Nripendra Narayan Bhup Bahadur, Maharaja of Cooch Behar

extremely popular grandson Jagaddipendra Narayan (1915–1970), nicknamed "Bhaya", led Bengal in the Ranji Trophy in the 1940s.The

grounds of the Maharaja of Cooch Behar's at Woodlands in Alipore and Maharaja of Natore's Natore Park at Ballygunge in Picnic Gardens, were exquisitely laid out in the manner of the best grounds in England. The lush green turf blended very well with the pines, the poplars and the firs that encircled the arenas.

The influence of cricket in this part of the country, then undivided Bengal, extended

Jagaddipendra Narayan, nicknamed "Bhaya"

to places as far as Natore, Murapara, Narayanganj, Mymensingh, Bikrampur, Dacca, Rangpur (now all in Bangladesh), Cooch Behar in North Bengal and Jorhat in upper Assam. In fact, the first-ever organized cricket tournament in the world for school children was held at Mymensingh (now in Bangladesh) in the 1880s.

House of Natore

Cricket by the turn of the 20th century was becoming very popular with the princely states. The Indian rajas and nawabs realized that cricket did make an immediate impact in their relationship with the colonial British rulers. Although *"shikar"* was their prime sporting activity at the time, some of these native rulers began to encourage cricket in their territory.

If Patiala and Cooch Behar were the pioneers, the native states of Holkar, Nawanagar, Baroda, Cochin and Travancore were not far behind. They raised their own teams, got coaches from abroad and also recruited players from England and Australia to strengthen their teams. However, the Maharaja of Natore (now in Bangladesh) was a glorious exception.

Jagadindra Nath Roy, the Maharaja of Natore

Jagadindra Nath Roy (1868 – 1925) the Maharaja of Natore would not even visualize having anything to do with talents borrowed from abroad. His team had only Indians playing.

The magnanimous patron would have Indians coming from all over the country and from all communities. What a visionary he was. Most of the top cricketers of India who went to UK with Patiala's XI in 1911 were from the Natore XI. Natore's ground was in the Picnic Garden area on the eastern periphery of Calcutta. Once Ranjitsinhji played here for the visiting Jamnagar side, while Palvankar Baloo was with Natore XI.

Once at a match an opposing captain leading Calcutta Cricket Club (CCC) asked Maharaja Jagadindra Nath Roy the number of pros in his side implying that there was no credit in beating CCC with

Natore Cricket Team: Palvankar Baloo and Jagadindra Nath Roy, the Maharaja of Natore seated 1st and 2nd from left in the middle row

hired players. The Maharaja promptly replied that since he himself did nothing else but play cricket, apart from he there was no other pro in his team. What a marvellous idea of giving respect to cricketers.

Ironically in the history of Indian cricket, this genuine patriot has been totally overlooked.

Porbandar & Limbdi

In 1932 the Indian cricket team set sail for Britain to play their first-ever official Test match. The chosen captain of the touring team was the Maharaja of Porbandar, Natwarsinhji (1901–1979). His deputy was the Maharaja of Limbdi, Ghanashyamsinhji (1902–1964).

Both were very average cricketers. But at the time, in the 1930s, it was felt that captains could only come from the princely classes. Hence the two members of the

Rana Natwarsinhji of Porbandar

royalty were given the top two posts in the Indian cricket team to play their debut Test.

Thankfully both Natwarsinhji and Ghanashyamsinhji were educated, liberal souls, in the most appropriate sense of those words. They were sensible enough to understand that if they were in the playing XI, the national team would become weak. Both declined to play in the inaugural Test at Lord's. That Test match being the sole Test of the series, they never got to play for India again.

Skipper Natwarsinhji and his deputy Ghanashyamsinhji decided that the best choice to lead would be the 'commoner' CK Nayudu. Accordingly, India's first-ever Test captain was Cottariya Konkaiya Nayudu, a magnificent all-rounder and a born leader of men. CK's elevation to the top was not because of the selection committee, but because of the magnanimous gesture of two princely gentlemen.

The chief reasons for highlighting this extraordinary event are quite a few. To begin with, this particular issue has not yet seen the light of day. Indian authors and historians could not decipher the magnitude of the gesture of two men who sacrificed immortality for the just cause of the nation. Both Natwarsinhji and Ghanashyamsinhji deserve our salute.

The 1932 Indian Test Cricket team that toured England. Middle row seated: Ghanashyamsinhji (Vice-captain), Maharaja of Porbandar, Natwarsinhji (captain)and C. K. Nayudu seated 4th, 3rd and 2nd respectively from left

Secondly, in the annals of international Test cricket such a unique sacrifice has never been seen. No captain-elect has ever relinquished his debut captaincy in this magnificent manner.

Thirdly, this is a very significant issue in the light of modern thinking. At a time when 'commoners' in BCCI are fighting among themselves for every bit of crumb on the table, we in India have had 'royal' people who knew how to sacrifice self for the cause of the deserving individuals as well as for the nation.

Natwarsinhji and Ghanashyamsinhji are names that even the top Indian cricketers and administrators are unaware of. In fact, they do not want to know about them. As one former supposedly, erudite India captain has recently observed, "...why bother about what happened earlier; all that is in the past!"

Today where is the time for chivalry and magnanimity in the quagmire of corruption? Now the whole emphasis is on money and power; power and money. Nothing else matters. Genuine cricket connoisseurs would do well to remember these unheralded and forgotten gentlemen of Indian cricket.

Worst of Royalty: Vizianagram, Nawanagar, Kathiawar and Iftikar Ali Khan Pataudi

Vijaya Anand 'Vizzy'

We mentioned about the magnanimity of Natwarsinhji and Ghanashyamsinhji, the respective maharajas of Porbandar and Limbdi, on the tour of Britain in 1932. We also discussed the extraordinary cricket ability of another 'royalty', Yadavendra Singh (1913–1974), the Yuvraj of Patiala.

We also covered the outstanding contribution to Indian cricket of the Maharaja of Cooch Behar, Nripendra Narayan and the Maharaja of Natore, Jagadindra Nath Roy. While on the subject of royal personages in Indian cricket, let us concentrate on other 'royal' personalities at the other extreme.

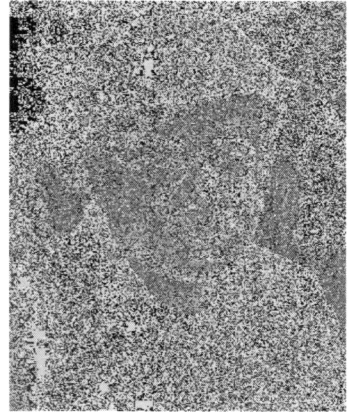

Maharajkumar of Vizianagram, Gajapati Vijaya Anand Raju, popularly known as Vizzy

On India's tour to England in 1936 the picture of 'Indian royalty' was completely reversed. This time the captain-elect was the Maharajkumar of Vizianagram, Gajapati Vijaya Anand Raju (1906–1965), popularly known as Vizzy. Vizzy fancied himself to be a capable cricketer, although he had no result to show his prowess as a batsman or as a captain. He manipulated the powers-that-be to such an extent that the selectors actually announced his name as the captain of the India team to tour Britain in 1936.

He played in all the three Tests in England thereby weakening the national team. His was a disastrous influence on the team. Incident after incident marred the 1936 tour: the Lala Amarnath fiasco; the controversial selection of Baqa Jilani and the Mushtaq–Merchant attempted conspiracy.

Lala Amarnath began the 1936 tour with his breezy style of cricket. He was doing exceptionally well with the bat as well as with the ball. In the match against the Minor Counties, skipper Vizzy kept changing Amarnath's batting order repeatedly. Amarnath, all padded-up and ready to bat, was fuming at the insulting scenario. He threw down his bat and used some choicest Punjabi slang.

The manager, an Englishman by the name of Brittain-Jones, and the captain Vizzy made a big hue and cry over the incident and ordered Amarnath to pack his bag and go back to India! Some well-meaning players approached the captain and the manager to forgive the young and impressionable Amarnath. But to no avail. He was sent back from the tour just prior to the start of the Test series. Lala Amarnath went into cricket history as the first Test cricketer to face such humiliation. Later a thorough enquiry was

Baqa Jilani. Jilani played his only Test in 1936 during a tour wrecked by infighting between two factions supportive of the captain Vizzy and the former captain C. K. Nayudu. Jilani belonged to the former group. A few days before the Test Match at the Oval, Jilani publicly insulted Nayudu while coming down to breakfast. It has been alleged that he owed to this incident his subsequent Test debut, a forgettable affair to which he contributed sixteen runs and fifteen wicketless overs. During the tour, according to Cota Ramaswami, Jilani suffered from high blood pressure, insomnia, sleep-walking and violent outbursts of temper. "Nobody could say when he was normal and when he got into uncontrollable temper. He was constantly undergoing treatment during the tour"

conducted, the BCCI absolved Lala Amarnath of all charges and he was back in the India team.

While Mushtaq Ali and Vijay Merchant were involved in a big opening partnership in the Manchester Test and going great guns, skipper Vizzy actually requested Mushtaq to run out Merchant! Mushtaq Ali related this incident in his autobiography *Cricket Delightful*. Mushtaq, of course, declined to carry out the strange request. In the process he lost out on a gold-plated wrist watch as gift from Vizzy!

Just before the 3rd and final Test at the Oval, skipper Vizzy offered a Test place to whoever would abuse and insult his main player CK Nayudu in public! Successful fast bowler Shute Banerjee – an educated, liberal persona – was the first to receive the offer! Obviously enough, he refused point-blank to do the dastardly job.

Unfortunately, another fast bowler Baqa Jilani took up the offer, gave a mouthful to CK Nayudu just a few days before the Test match and went on to make his debut at the Oval. Shute Banerjee, a man of strict principles, with far superior performance on the tour, was omitted from the XI because he did not curse and humiliate CK!

This was Indian cricket at the time. Not that the scenario is much better now: the omission of Amol Muzumder is a sad, contemporary issue.

Two extremes, perpetually as it were, running parallel to one another. Unfortunately, we have not bothered to herald the magnanimous, selfless gesture of Natwarsinhji and Ghanashyamsinhji but have remembered Vizzy's disgraceful nature! Strange are the ways of cricket and cricketers in India.

However, in all fairness to Vizzy, we must readily acknowledge his contribution to Indian cricket. He was a very sincere patron of cricket. He was genuinely devoted towards the game. He had his own team and organized matches in various cities. Spent generously on cricket and cricketers. Even went to the extent of inviting Sir Jack Hobbs and

Herbert Sutcliffe to India to play for his invitational team around the sub-continent.

But to give credence to his dream — the ambition to lead India — the man's manipulative efforts spoilt his reputation forever. The national selectors at the time were HD Kanga and the two 'royals' Iftikar Ali Khan Pataudi and KS Duleepsinhji. By their bias towards undeserving royalty, they too did not cover themselves with any credit as national selectors. Prominent men, best of formal schooling, former cricketers of renown yet their prejudicial minds set back Indian cricket by several years.

In later years Vizzy's was a constant presence on All India Radio as a commentator. Well-versed in the history of cricket and its folklore, Vizzy regaled his listeners with his remarkable memory.

I personally would prefer to remember Vizzy as a great patron of Indian cricket and as an erudite commentator. How I wish he had gone with the 1936 Indian team to England as manager and not as captain.

Pradumansinhji and BB Nimbalkar

The small territory of Kathiawar based in the western part of India in the Gujarat peninsula had a ruler whose heart was as small as the land he governed. He was known as the Thakore Sahab of Rajkot, Pradumansinhji.

Kathiawar was included among the teams for the Ranji Trophy championship in the season 1948–49. The Kathiawar cricket team travelled to Poona to play against the might of Maharashtra at the Poona Gymkhana ground, which was known to be a bowler's graveyard. Mammoth totals were recorded on this ground over the years.

BB Nimbalkar - Only Indian to score a quadruple ton in first-class cricket

Winning the toss, the Kathiawar captain Pradumansinhji decided to take the first strike. Considering the reputation of the docile pitch, newcomers Kathiawar recorded an unimpressive total of 236, which included a dashing 77 by the skipper.

When Maharashtra came to bat one could feel the difference in strength and strategy between the two teams. While the debutant Kathiawaris appeared disoriented and the leadership hesitant, Maharashtra adopted the no-nonsense approach as exemplified by their mentor-captain-guru combined, Prof Dinkar Balwant Deodhar.

The two openers, MR Rege and Kamal Bhandarkar attacked the weak opposition bowling from the beginning and raced to 81 when Rege left. Now, the prolific Ranji Trophy run-getter BB Nimbalkar appeared on the scene with his trademark handkerchief around his neck.

Bhandarkar and Nimbalkar added a world record score of 455 runs for the 2nd wicket in just 300 minutes. After Bhandarkar (205) left, 'Bhao Sahab' Nimbalkar continued with his judicious stroke-play. When Nimbalkar's individual score had reached 443, the Kathiawar captain Pradumansinhji announced that his team would not take further part in the match.

Nimbalkar was on 443 just 9 runs short of Sir Donald Bradman's the then world record of 452. It was a most unsportsmanlike decision on the part of the Kathiawar captain, Pradumansinhji, who happened to be a distant relative of Ranjitsinhji.

Nimbalkar was denied a world record by his own countryman. It appears that so enamoured was Pradumansinhji by the supposed 'superiority' of white-skinned people that he did not want a fellow Indian to overhaul the white man's achievement.

Just goes to show that 'royals' are no different from people who are not born with the supposed 'blue' blood. They have the same weaknesses, same mean-mindedness, similar failings as the commoners. Magnanimity, humility, integrity have nothing to do with one's financial background or academic accomplishments.

Nawanagar's Strange Decision Regarding Shute Banerjee

In the Ranji Trophy championship the erstwhile princely territory of Nawanagar has an enviable record. Apart from Bombay no other team has been able to do what Nawanagar did in the 1936–37 season. Nawanagar won the championship in their first year of participation as Bombay had done in the inaugural season in 1934–35.

The Nawanagar State team played in the Ranji Trophy championship in the 1930s and 1940s. The team was disbanded at the time of independence when the princely States joined the Indian Union. The Nawanagar State employed many top cricketers of India and generally promoted the game in their own territory.

Author with former Test cricketer Shute Banerjee, the East Zone team manager, 1973

In Nawanagar's first venture into the national championship, they won the coveted Ranji Trophy at Bombay's Brabourne Stadium in 1936–37 defeating Bengal in the final. They had a strong outfit with the outstanding Amar Singh supported by the highly talented youngster Vinoo Mankad. The magnificent all-rounder Salim Durani's father Abdul Aziz happened to be the wicket-keeper of the team.

Shute Banerjee

Although three princes played for Nawanagar – Indravijayasinhji, Yadvendrasinhji and Ranvirsinhji – very sensibly the captaincy was bestowed upon the experienced and prolific Sussex all-rounder, Albert Frederick Wensley. Wensley became the first professional English County cricketer to play in the Ranji Trophy championship.

However, Nawanagar resorted to a highly unethical practice in the recruitment of the India all-rounder Shute Banerjee. Banerjee had gone to Bombay with the Bengal team, his home State, to play against Nawanagar in the Ranji Trophy final. As the premier all-rounder, he was having a highly successful season for Bengal.

On the eve of the match, the Nawanagar State offered Shute Banerjee a job with the condition that he had to join their service from the next morning itself, which happened to be the first day of the Ranji Trophy final! The offer was couched in such a manner that Banerjee would not be able to play against Nawanagar.

The unemployed, young all-rounder Banerjee was in a quandary. He had little option. He opted for the security of a job thereby rendering himself ineligible for the final against Nawanagar. Those days the rules of BCCI were highly elastic and inevitably some elements took advantage of the situation. Thus, Bengal was deprived of their main player and Nawanagar went on to win the Ranji Trophy with comparative ease.

The Bengal captain was PI Van der Gucht, a wicket-keeper of Dutch descent. He spoke to his opposing counterpart, AF Wensley, regarding the strange and unusual scenario, but without any success. Wensley pleaded helplessness as the 'orders' had come from the State monarch.

Just goes to show that the so-called 'spirit of cricket' was sacrificed with impunity even in the past as it is done today. Officials and players of the past were no saints. In fact, in the earlier days, conspiracies and back-stabbing were as common as those are today.

Iftikar Ali Khan Pataudi (1910–1952)

At the conclusion of the war, in 1946 India set off for her 3rd official Test tour of England. The mood in the Indian cricket circles was very optimistic. India had just won a series against Lindsay Hasset's Australian Services team. Although it was only an unofficial Test series and that too against a non-representative Aussie side, yet there were enough reasons for Indians to feel encouraged.

Iftikar Ali Khan, the senior Nawab of Pataudi with Wally Hammond during the 1946 England tour

Young talents had emerged in the form of Vijay Hazare, Vinoo Mankad, Rusi Modi and Abdul Hafeez Kardar. And the veterans too like Vijay Merchant, Mushtaq Ali and Lala Amarnath were also in the pink of cricketing health. During the War years when hardly any cricket was played in England, cricket in India went on uninterrupted and the players were hungry for success at the international level.

For the 1946 tour of England the captaincy crown was certain to be on the cool head of Vijay Merchant who had done a wonderful job on the tour of Sri Lanka as well as against Australian Services, both the series being in 1945. But true to our whimsical ways, some influential BCCI members felt that on the tour of England it was imperative that the captain should be of 'royal blood'!

This strange reasoning had played havoc with India's prospects on the two previous tours to England in 1932 and in 1936. Maharaja of Porbandar, Natwarsinhji and Vijaya Anand, the Maharajkumar of Vizianagram, both average club-level players, were the official captains.

The Indian Cricket Team during the 1946 tour of England

Now in 1946 the name of Nawab of Pataudi Iftikar All Khan was raised. No doubt that Iftikar Ali Khan Pataudi had impeccable cricketing credentials. He was an exceptionally gifted cricketer, who had scored a Test debut century for England against Australia.

But that was way back, almost 14 years ago in 1932–33 when he was a talented youth of 22. Since then he had played only occasionally, and in 1946 his form and fitness hardly warranted his selection, not even as a player. Yet the powerful lobbies got their job done and Iftikar Ali Khan Pataudi, much to the surprise and annoyance of most cricket addicts and players, accepted the responsibility of leading India to England in the summer of 1946.

Why did Pataudi do so is a matter of surprise. Here was a level-headed man who should have realized that at 36 his best days were long over. He had hardly played any cricket since the late 1930s. Why did he opt to lead India is an issue of serious conjecture? Was it because he had never led India in official Tests? Did he put his personal interest ahead of his national interest? Whatever be the reasons, he did himself no credit.

Actually, he was one of the selectors of the national team in the mid-1930s! From being a selector to decide to become a player once again when he was neither physically fit nor capable enough was a sacrilege, nothing less. It was a serious blemish on his part, a problem which left behind a legacy of poor leadership.

The War had just ended. Hardly any serious cricket was possible in England in the War years. Rationing of food was on and the facilities minimal. Despite innumerable obstacles, Wally Hammond and his England team won the series against India by 2 matches to nil with relative ease because of weak leadership and partisan selection policy.

Skipper Pataudi was an abject failure in the Tests, as was only to be expected. His batting was only a pale, indistinct shadow of the early 1930s. In 5 innings he scored 55 runs for an average of 11. Fitter and superior players sat on the sidelines as victims of 'royal' discrimination.

Ironically, a top-quality cricketer of Pataudi's eminence shattered his own image, exactly as a club-level batsman like Vizzy had done a decade back. Both Vizzy and Pataudi placed their personal ambitions ahead of their respective team's interest. They cared little that by their presence as captains they were weakening the national team.

Ranjitsinhji (1872–1933): An Enigma?

Ranji never played a Christian stroke in his life. So observed Sir Neville Cardus, the doyen of cricket writers. True it was. No structured, conventional rationality interrupted Ranji's spontaneous rhythm on the field. The Indian prince's batsmanship had all the charms of Oriental mysticism. The bat was his wand as he mesmerized England, both spectators and oppositions, with his wristy elegance and twinkling footwork.

In an era when the top batters of the world would play the ball mainly to the off-side as the 'Champion' WG Grace would do with his customary mastery,

Ranji

the graceful, lissom figure of Ranji would gently caress the ball from outside the off-stump to the untenanted areas on the leg-side. It was heresy. Die-hard critics of the game shook their heads in disbelief. It could not happen again and again, they thought. But then it did happen again and again. It was sheer magic: coordination of eye and mind; feet and bat. None before had done it.

How did he do it with a perpendicular-held bat? With a cross bat, we understand. But how with a bat held straight? He was the first to use the pace of the ball to glance it between the fine-leg and square-leg regions. The fluidity of his steely wrists gave the art of batsmanship a new dimension.

Moustachioed and ebony of complexion, the traits of his race were distinctly apparent in this conjuror's every step. Medium of height,

shining black hair thinning on the temples the man looked every inch an Oriental. Yet he was giving the white man a lesson in effortless stroke execution at the white man's own sport. Who is he? What are his antecedents? How is he lighting up our grey skies with his golden streak? These were the queries in the minds of cricket followers from Yorkshire to Sussex.

Kumar Shri Ranjitsinhji was the adopted son of the Raja of Nawanagar, who had no male heir to his throne. Following the best possible education on offer in India, Ranji went to England for further studies with his school headmaster in tow. Cambridge was the university chosen.

The climate and the food disagreed with the prince brought up in India. He was overwhelmed by the liberal western culture that he daily encountered. Perplexed he was by the differences. After the initial hiccups, he however found his métier in the game of cricket. He had played a little at school in India but in England in the game of cricket he found an ideal escape route from the dreary routine of academic life.

His soft features belied his determination. He spent hours practicing at the nets. The young prince went for the trials of the Cambridge University cricket team. But he returned disappointed as players of far superior ability got the nod ahead of him. He realized that he would have to work really hard if he wanted to be in the first XI. And that is exactly what he did.

He appointed professional coaches, who would bowl to him for hours against payment. As a bonus he would keep a silver coin on the stumps for the bowlers to aim at. Whoever was successful in 'castling' Ranji at the net session would be the recipient of the coin!

What an innovation to think of. What an incentive for the hard-working, ill-paid, professional bowlers of the late 19th century. This was his distinctive style of encouraging the bowlers, which was later emulated by some others without giving the originator Ranji the credit for the innovative incentive.

The Indian prince never tried to copy WG Grace or Arthur Shrewsbury, the immaculate role models at the time. Very sensibly he developed a distinctive style of his own. He did not go for power; he went for precision. He used his wrists more than he used his forearms. While others tried to play on the off side, he preferred to play on the leg side. He picked up the tenets of back-foot play from WG but avoided the cross-batted shots.

Ranji's mastery was finally acknowledged. He was selected for Cambridge University, later invited to play for Sussex and finally for England in the Manchester Test in 1896 against Australia. He began his Test career with a century for England against Australia. He sent spectators and the journalists into raptures. They were amazed to see the man's effortless mastery over pace and spin. No condition would upset him. No opposition would overawe him.

He was majestic in whatever he did. He had all the Oriental flavour of mysticism around him. Silk shirt and cream flannels fluttering in the breeze, he gave the impression of effortless ease. His strokes conveyed the essence and not the effort. He strode supreme and earned universal admiration. Ranjitsinhji, who later became the Jamsahib of Nawanagar, was popularly known as 'Smith' during his Cambridge University days.

Unfortunately for Indian cricket, Ranji had no time for his motherland. He had a very poor opinion of Indian cricket and Indian cricketers. He played a few matches in India but never showed any interest in promoting the game here. At Eden Gardens he once played a match as well as another at Natore Park in the Picnic Garden district of Ballygunge in south Calcutta.

Very surprisingly, even the grand exploits on English soil of Mehallasha Pavri (for the Parsees) and Palvankar Baloo (for the Patiala's Indians), who were so highly rated by discerning British critics who saw them in action in England, did not quite wake up Ranji from his stupor. He just could not visualize that other Indians could also be world-beaters.

Amazing attitude, indeed, for a man who was brought up on liberal, western education.

He seemed quite oblivious to the progress that was happening in India. The quality of the Triangular and Quadrangular communal cricket tournaments had no appeal for him. He had no praise for DB Deodhar or for CK Nayudu, even when they were so successful against Arthur Gilligan's visiting MCC side of 1926. In fact, the magnificent all-rounder Amar Singh Ladla was from Nawanagar, Ranji's own territory, yet the grand ol' man never offered even any words of encouragement to him.

Ranji's strange conduct in relation to Indian cricket defied all logic. Why was the great cricketer so adamant in his opposition to the march of Indian cricket? No one will ever know. Ranji's biographer Simon Wilde did not give high marks to Ranji as a person. Much less of Ranji as a ruler. Actually, he trashed many of the Ranji-related eulogies of the earlier authors.

When Ranjitsinhji's nephew, Duleepsinhji – another outstanding batsman – was invited to play Test matches for India in 1932, it was reported that Ranji flatly refused to give permission by saying that Duleep would not play as he was an English Test cricketer!

Yes, Duleepsinhji had made his debut for England against South Africa in 1929 and later scored a century against Australia at Lord's the following summer. He could have easily served his motherland in India's early days at Test cricket in the 1930s. But he had no desire to defy the dictates of his stern uncle, whom he obviously idolized.

When the inauguration of the national championship was being discussed at the

Duleepsinhji

BCCI meeting, the Maharaja of Patiala, Bhupendra Singh announced that he would donate the trophy and the trophy would be named after Ranjitsinhji, who had just expired. Unfortunately, Indian cricket writers have never acknowledged the magnanimity of Patiala and the BCCI members of the time.

Ironically Ranji, who could have done so much, kept himself totally away from Indian cricket and cricketers. Being very close to the ruling class of Britons, he could have been a great help to Indian cricket in its early days. On account of his cricket exploits in England, he was also very popular with the Indian princes and ruling elites. He had power and influence. He had all the credentials to move mountains. But not once did he show any inclination to come to the aid of Indian cricket in any way.

Phenomenal are his statistical embellishments, both in England as well as in Australia. Despite losing an eye in a shooting accident in India, he played for a while for Sussex. Later he represented India at the League of Nations. His close friend the devastatingly handsome Charles Burgess Fry – probably the greatest of all academic-sportsmen – was his constant companion on and off the field.

Although Fry's exceptional qualities influenced the Rajput ruler of Nawanagar in many ways, it is indeed surprising that Ranji could not bring himself to assist Indian cricket in its hour of need. CB Fry, who guided a whole generation of students over the years in diverse activities, ultimately could not make his closest friend take a single step for the betterment of Indian cricket.

Charles Burgess Fry

It was indeed a grand gesture on the part of the Patiala House and the BCCI members of the early 1930s to honour the magnificent batsman who first put India on the world cricket map. It was also ironical that a man who never encouraged Indian cricket or Indian cricketers would be given the highest possible acclaim. Strange are the ways of Indian cricket. Stranger still was the conduct of Ranji.

Behind the Scene

Ambanis, Gandhis and NKP Salve

Dhirubhai Ambani's patriotism in the cause of cricket

Dhirubhai Ambani was posthumously honoured by the Government of India with the coveted award of Padma Vibhushan for his unparalleled contribution to the Indian industrial environment. The sheer magnitude of Dhirubhai's achievement in the industrial sector has dwarfed many of his other stupendous work in the interest of Indian society.

Dhirubhai Ambani joining the celebrations with Allan Border after the final of Reliance World Cup 1987 held at Eden Gardens, Kolkata

One of his magnificent achievements is in the arena of cricket. Sadly, the issue has never been highlighted in our country. His yeoman contribution to cricket has never been acknowledged and recognized.

Dhirubhai Ambani happens to be among the eminent visionaries who gave cricket in India a new and novel dimension. He exemplified the spirit of patriotism in no uncertain manner on a monsoon morn in Mumbai way back in1983. He picked up the phone receiver and gave his assent as the voice from the prime minister's office informed him to meet the prime minister within a couple of days.

The visionary industrialist did not have a single query. Nor did he want to know the reason for the urgency. Dhirubhai wasted no time. Next day he was at Mrs. Indira Gandhi's chamber at 10 Janpath in New Delhi to keep his appointment as desired by the prime minister herself.

NKP Salve, the president of the Board of Control for Cricket in India, was also asked by the PMO to be present in the room at the appointed hour. Salve happened to be a cabinet minister at the time and was very highly rated for his integrity as a lawyer as well as a politician.

Prime minister Mrs. Gandhi kept the usual pleasantries short, as was her style, and went straight into the principal issue. She asked Dhirubhai whether the latter would be keen to sponsor a world cricket championship on Indian soil.

Indira Gandhi

Dhirubhai Ambani, God bless him, did not hesitate for a moment. Instantly he realized that the image and prestige of his nation was at stake. He nodded and uttered, "Madam, yes, I would be too happy to give a blank cheque to cover the entire cost of the tournament since it is for a national cause."

He did not betray any emotion. He asked no questions. He sought no clarifications. The patriot in him immediately grasped that the money was to be spent to uphold India's honour. For him that was enough reason. He offered a blank cheque. Yes, that was Dhirubhai Ambani. This is a glorious example of how politicians and industrialists can come forward for the cause of the country through the popular medium of sports.

But we are going ahead of the actual story. The story begins at Lord's. June 25, 1983 to be precise. India had reached the Prudential World Cup final against all odds. "Kapil's Devils" were to play the defending champions, the rampaging West Indies at the Lord's.

A few days prior to the final, just after India had defeated the hosts England in the semi-final, the BCCI president NKP Salve requested the authorities at the Lord's for 2 tickets for the final. The tickets were requested for Siddhartha Shankar Ray and his wife Maya. SS Ray, a former Calcutta University Cricket Blue, was at the time the Indian High Commissioner to USA.

Surprisingly the authorities at the Lord's turned down the request of the BCCI president. Even priced tickets were not made available. For Salve, the epitome of gentlemanliness, this was an embarrassing scenario. The president of one of the finalist teams could not offer just two tickets to an Indian ambassador. NKP Salve, man of high integrity and self-respect, decided there and then that he would not take this insult to his country lying down.

When India won the coveted trophy, the president of BCCI NKP Salve lost no time and brought the winning team over to New Delhi from Heathrow to meet the prime minister. After the reception was over, Salve made a beeline for Mrs. Gandhi and told her of the humiliation that he had to face in London over those two tickets.

NKP Salve

Mrs. Gandhi asked Salve what he had contemplated to avenge the insult. Salve, the outstanding lawyer and clever politician, had a mind of his own. He devised that he would try to get the world cup out of the clutches of England who had monopolized hosting quadrennial tournament since 1975.

Within the course of the next few months the BCCI was keeping itself prepared to take on the challenges of the major cricketing powers of the time, England and Australia. It was decided that at the next meeting of the ICC, where the dates of the following world cup in England would be decided, the BCCI would offer double the guarantee money to all the participating teams. On the day of the meeting at Lord's, true to form, the plan was executed to perfection.

At the ICC meeting held at the Lord's to confirm England as host, the eloquence of NKP Salve had the influential lobbies scurrying for cover. In a magnanimous gesture, the BCCI president doubled the guarantee money if the tournament was held in India and then, for good measure, made some more concessions for the benefit of the players and their families. All reservations about playing the world cup on Indian soil evaporated into thin air in next to no time.

The ultimate decision of the meeting heralded that the 1987 edition of the world cup would be held in India. In another master-stroke of diplomacy, the statesman in NKP Salve asked Pakistan to be a co-host. The 1987 world cup was the first world cup in cricket to vanquish the monopoly of England as the permanent venue. Since then the world cup championship keeps moving around the globe by rotation as it should be in a democratic scenario.

The spirit displayed by Dhirubhai Ambani, NKP Salve and Mrs. Gandhi has been forgotten in this land of ours. They showed the way how politicians, professionals and industrialists can help to shape the world through the medium of sports. But the juggernaut, massive and strong, was too good to last. Mrs. Gandhi was assassinated in October 1984. The country was in turmoil. The world cup was only of secondary importance. Obviously enough, there were far more important jobs awaiting attention.

But Salve had other ideas. He approached Dhirubhai to find out if he was still willing to sponsor the world cup. Salve's apprehension can well be imagined. Indira Gandhi was no more. The nation was staring at a crisis after a crisis. But the industrialist from Mumbai said, "Nothing doing, the show must go on. I will not go back on my word." As promised, the blank cheque from Dhirubhai Ambani remained with BCCI's Salve.

Rajiv Gandhi took over from his late mother. Salve kept his unwavering focus. On his part, the patriot Dhirubhai, who had no interest in sports, sent his younger son Anil to get involved with the staging of the world cup. In one grand gesture of magnanimity, Anil Ambani had all the cricket boards salivating.

Anil offered complimentary hospitality to all the office bearers of the respective cricket boards. This was purposely done just to add salt to England's wound. People who had denied India just two tickets were granted full hospitality throughout the course of the championship! It was an exemplary Gandhian master-stroke by the Reliance owner.

The trio – Salve, Ambani and Gandhi – was magnificent in handling the global event. The Reliance Cup was an outstanding success in terms of media coverage, sponsorship and crowd participation. Just goes to show that with the right people in right places, India can move the world. Dhirubhai Ambani deserves our salute for his superlative, patriotic gesture.

Russy Mody: The Man Who Genuinely Respected Sportspeople

The first patrons of Indian sports were the Princely States of the pre-independence era. Later Indian Railways and the Services were very magnanimous to offer employment to talented sportsmen.

From the 1950s some private sector companies, particularly in Mumbai and Chennai, took the initiative to recruit talented sportsmen. But the corporate entity that genuinely went into promoting various sports disciplines and sportsmen were the Tata's. The principal catalyst was an executive by the name of Russy Mody.

Russy Mody

Grace and graciousness flowed in his veins. At Jamshedpur in 1972 when East Zone was billed to play the visiting England team led by Tony Lewis, Russy Mody came to meet the East Zone players at the nets the previous afternoon. As he walked into the Keenan Stadium, dressed in a floral-print Hawaiian shirt and loose Bermudas, the players, officials and the groundsmen rushed towards him, but he waved them away saying, "No, no, carry on with the net session. I shall wait till the end."

He kept his word. He did not walk on to the ground. He did not try to show he was the boss of the place. He just sat on a cane chair on the periphery and chatted with Sudhir Das, the prominent Bihar all-rounder of yesteryears who happened to be our cricket manager at the time.

As we finished our net practice and walked back towards the pavilion, he came and introduced himself to us with a smile, "I am your host for the match. Any problems you have, just let Sudhir know about it." Exchanged pleasantries with all the players, most of the senior cricketers were well known to him. Before departing, casually mentioned, "Since you are playing against an international team, please think you are representing India."

For a 22-year old debutant, this was a highly motivating message to me. He sounded so simple and easy. Made us feel relaxed. His modesty was unbelievable. Not once did he create any impression of high office. Not once did he try to create an overbearing scenario. He actually had tea with us in an earthen *bhaar*, as was the custom at the grounds in those days. Even dunked a biscuit in the tea before biting into it, in typical Indian fashion. Personally, I took an instant liking for the man's easy manner.

Russy Mody was a multi-dimensional persona. Like a true industrialist, he thought of social welfare through community service as early as the 1960s. He worshipped cricket yet spent time and effort on every other sports discipline. His sponsorship of social welfare activities never came to the fore. He was at ease with ministers as he was with the *chai-walas* on the street.

At Digwadih in the coal belt of Jamadoba, near Dhanbad in erstwhile Bihar (now Jharkhand), where the Tata's had their collieries, he engaged a first-class cricketer, Kalyan Mitter, as a curator to prepare a cricket ground. Later Daljit Singh and Robin Mukherjea, two renowned cricketers, followed to prepare facilities for football, hockey, volleyball and other disciplines.

His thoughts centred on the welfare of the children of coal-miners! The massive projects were being carried out to help these deprived youngsters to find an avenue for their personal development. Mr. Mody, the magnanimous visionary, chose sports because he realized the appeal of sports to children of all ages and status. Sorry to add that even now in India we have not realized the importance of sports. We are only concerned about the enormous revenue that sports generate. Nothing else.

In the 1970s Russy Mody would invite international cricketers of the calibre of Salim Durani, Hanumant Singh and Dilip Sardesai, among others, to take part in the Homi Mody cricket championship at Digwadih Stadium. The tournament was held in September-October, at a time when no cricket was possible in any other part of eastern India because of the extended rainy season.

This was the place where the East Zone players would get some practice matches before the start of the domestic season. Many young cricketers began their career because of Russy Mody's benevolence. This writer happens to be one of them.

In time, many prominent names of Indian football, hockey and volleyball came up from the coal-mining districts of Jamadoba and Jealgora. All this was possible because of one man who refused take any credit or publicity for his generosity or for his vision.

From the mid-1970s, Russy Mody XI would go around the country to play various tournaments. Amazingly along with ten players from Bihar there would be one from Bengal in his combined team. He never quite forgot me.

I once approached him for a job. The immediate response was, "Of course. You like to write. I think you should join our public relations department at Jamshedpur." I replied, "But, sir, I am leading Bengal and cannot afford to leave Calcutta now." He smiled and said, "Ra-jew (that's how he pronounced my name), you would be better off in Bihar than in Bengal." He was absolutely right. I wish I had taken the plunge.

He lived life to the full. And expected others to do so as well. He patronized sportspeople like the maharajas of old. He would allow them full freedom to play and to work. He wanted people to develop themselves. Magnanimity escorted him wherever he went. So much so that scores of people took advantage of his generosity. Yet not once did he ever show any remorse or regret.

For such a great lover of cricket, ironically, he just could not put bat to ball. Totally non-athletic in frame, the hand and eye co-ordination lacked sporting prowess. He tried his hand at bowling and developed a peculiar way of delivering the ball. He would release the ball very early and the ball would go up for about 15 or so feet and descend on a spot near the batsman! The ball would lose almost all momentum on pitching and would more often than not drop 'dead' before reaching the batter!

But he had an ear for music. On his piano his fingers played the symphonies of Mozart and Beethoven to perfection. But throughout his life his first love remained cricket.

He was a genuine visionary. Today what is known in corporate circles as man-management was in his blood. He did not have to learn to be courteous. He did not have to resort to hypocrisy to impress or to draw attention. He never wanted publicity; never flaunted his friendship with the rich and the famous. To show off his 'personality and importance' he did not cocoon himself in a grave face.

On the contrary, the real Russy Mody was gregarious, soft-natured, polite and generous to a fault. He accepted all the trickery and back-stabbing over the years with a hearty laugh.

He was the person who established the football academy at Jamshedpur, where later other sports disciplines like athletics, archery and gymnastics among others prospered. After his untimely departure from Tata's, the academy lost its glamour and Jamshedpur lost its eminence as a centre of sports.

Russy Mody gave jobs to prominent sportsmen who served Tata's office teams in various states. His generosity extended even to physically handicapped former sportsmen who would not be able to play for the Tata office teams. But never, never would he beat his own drums in any platform. In fact, a journalist once recounted that it was almost impossible to get Russy Mody for an interview. He was easily accessible but too proactive to sit in one place and talk about himself. That was not in his genes.

Russy Mody met trade union leaders with a, "open-door" policy. One leftist union leader once recounted, "He would call all the union leaders of different camps together to discuss issues. There was never any separate meeting with any particular union. He did not believe in any hide-and-seek system. We respected and believed him totally. We knew he would never go back on his word."

Just prior to his death I met him at the Nagraj Bar of Bengal Club in Calcutta. Bowed low to him and before I could finish my sentence, "Sir, I know you have forgotten me," he raised his hand and softly said, "Rajew, no?" What do you make of this genius who had supposedly lost his memory?

After a few months, I was writing his obituary. Sent it to a leading Kolkata daily. They did not publish it apprehending repercussions as Russy Mody had suddenly resigned and left. Even in death, his legacy tormented the corrupt and the callous.

Ironically the very men who took advantage of Russy Mody kept a distance from him when he bade good-bye to the company he served for decades. Some avoided him in public. Others kept a discreet distance. Their very selfish considerations took control of their decisions.

But, even in private conversations, none could really say a word against him. Influential people very close to him when he was in power had no time for him when out of office. It mattered little to the short, bulky frame with the softest of eyes. He accepted the hypocrisy with extreme grace and a cultured demeanour.

His service to Indian sport has never been surpassed in contemporary times. With his passion for the game, his love for cricketers, his administrative skills and his unimpeachable integrity, he would have made a marvellous president of BCCI or any other sports federation including the Indian Olympic Association.

But he had no craving for power or for position. Certainly not a person to campaign or cajole. Most surely not a person to indulge in any rat-race. Never had any intention to flex muscles. No way would he use his massive popularity.

But our attitude is so hypocritical that we have forgotten the very man who first gave genuine prominence, social status, financial support and respect to performers of all sports disciplines.

No other Indian administrator has done as much for sports and sports-people as he has. He stands a singular sentinel for the cause of Indian sports.

Tests: Unofficial or Official?

Did WG Grace and KS Ranjitsinhji actually play Test cricket for England? The answer is a firm, no. No, they did not. If by Test cricket is meant playing representative cricket, then neither WG nor Ranji can be considered to be Test cricketers.

Both of them began and finished their careers before the birth of Imperial Cricket Conference (Now, International Cricket Council, or for short, ICC). WG's cricket career started with Gloucestershire County Cricket Club in the late 1870s. He and his two brothers were coached by their mother on the lawns of their bungalow at a small village near Bristol in Gloucestershire. All three brothers together played for an England XI at the Oval in 1880 against the visiting Australians. By no stretch of imagination were these representative matches. However, these matches

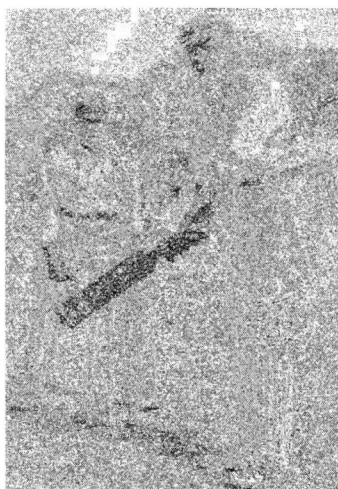

WG Grace

subsequently came to be rated by the cricket officialdom in England to be official Test matches, without any basis of justification.

The English teams for these matches were not chosen by any centralized cricket controlling body in England for the precise reason that there was no such body at the time. Nor did these matches have any recognition from any international authority, like the ICC, for the simple reason that no such organization existed at the time. Only as late as 1909 was the ICC established.

In England a body called The Board of Control for Test Cricket was formed in 1898 and a selection committee was appointed in 1899. The first Test in this series marked the end of WG's career. Thus, even if we decide to ignore the existence of ICC regarding the status of cricket matches as "Test Matches" and just satisfy ourselves with a national selection committee then Dr. WG Grace would be rated as a cricketer who played just one Test match. The match was held at Trent Bridge in Nottingham from 1st to 3rd June in 1899.

But even here, another problem would persist. In 1899 Australia did not have a centralized cricket control board with the authority to select the representative Australia side. So, the Australian players for that particular match were chosen not by their national selectors but by individuals on the basis of their own discretion. Thus, if we are to give "Test cricketer" status to WG, then we would have to give a similar status to the Australians also who played in that particular match and series. But this should not be for the sole and simple reason already mentioned that Australia lacked a cricket controlling body.

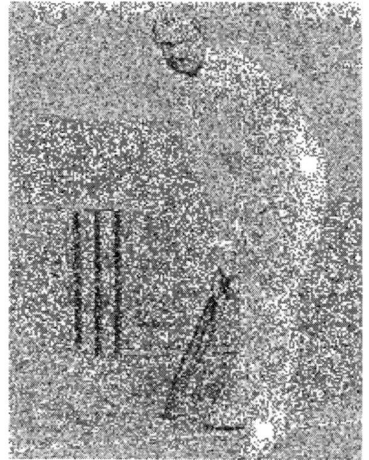

Ranji

Hence, for all practical purpose Dr. WG Grace, the great cricketer that he was, has to remain outside the domain of official Test Match cricket.

Similar is the case with Kumar Shri Ranjitsinhji. As the adopted child-heir to the throne of Nawanagar, he was taken to England by the headmaster of his school, an Englishman by the name of Chester Macnaghten. In England, he went up to Cambridge University as was the trend of the time among the children of princely and wealthy families.

Although Ranji was an Indian by birth and by no means qualified to play for England, yet we are choosing to ignore the point at this juncture. We are treating Ranji as an eligible candidate to represent England. Let us say, by virtue of his residence in UK and also because India did not have a national team at the time.

Now, to go back to our original contention: was Ranji a Test cricketer? Ranji's outstanding success in the summer of 1896 for Sussex in the county cricket championship could not be overlooked. He was by far the best batsman on form in England at the time.

In those days teams were not chosen by any national selection committee but by the individuals of the host club or county where the match was being played. The first Test in 1896 against Australia was scheduled at Lord's. The ground authorities at Lord's, who enjoyed the sole prerogative of team selection, did not consider Ranji for their England team at Lord's in 1896 for the 1st Test.

However, in the next match, the 2nd Test of the 1896 series at Old Trafford in Manchester, the local county authorities decided to select Ranji in the England final XI. Thus, Ranji made his Test debut at Manchester in the 2nd Test in the 1896 series against Australia. He scored a magnificent century on debut and the authorities in the following Test at the Oval too invited him to play on their ground in the 3rd Test. Although Ranji's high quality of batsmanship was in no doubt and that his was a very deserving selection, it must be admitted that not all the other members of those English teams were selected on merit but entirely on individual whims and fancies of the host county administrators.

In fact, the earlier English teams were not known as 'England' but as 'England XI'. This was certainly the most appropriate nomenclature. England's first national selection committee was appointed only in 1899. Australia's came into existence six years later in 1905. South Africa's centralized cricket control board emerged the earliest of the three nations in 1895. So, prior to these years, the teams of these countries were certainly not representative sides. The ICC as the controlling body for international cricket came to existence only in 1909.

Thus, it is conclusively proved that the era of official Test cricket should not commence from 1877 as is the conventional wisdom. But the beginning should be from 1909 with the formation of ICC. And that the great cricketers WG and Ranji cannot be considered to be official Test cricketers at all.

This issue is being highlighted for the simple reason that at the time prior to 1909 there was no international controlling authority to decide upon the status of official Test matches. These matches were not between representative sides but between teams chosen entirely on the basis of personal liking.

If, however we are to consider these Anglo-Australian matches as official Test matches, then why should the Aboriginals of Australia under Charles Lawrence, who first toured England in 1868 and gave an excellent account of themselves, be deprived of that status of being the first Test cricketers?

Moreover, by the same logic the Parsee teams of the 1880s and the Indian team to England of Maharaja of Patiala in 1911 should also be considered as official entities. And then players of the calibre of Mehallasha Pavri, Baloo Palvankar, Kekashru Maneksha Mistry (1874–1959) and others would become also official Test cricketers. And further Dinkar Balwant Deodhar's brilliant century against Gilligan's England (then MCC) would have to be regarded as India's first century in Test cricket.

In 1926 the first representative team to come to India from abroad was from England under Arthur Gilligan. The team comprising players from various

The first Indian team to tour England: The Parsi team in 1886

English County teams, under the nomenclature of MCC as was the trend of the time, came to play in India. Gilligan's men travelled around the sub-continent and played against the representative teams of the best possible 'national' players in combination.

One such match was held at Bombay in 1926, where the Marathi Sanskrit scholar from Poona, Professor Dinkar Balwant Deodhar, scored a magnificent 148. This happens to be the first-ever century by an Indian against a foreign representative team.

It is indeed most unfortunate to mention that Deodhar did not receive his rightful due. This match came to be regarded as unofficial as India then was not a member of ICC nor did India have a centralized cricket board. In the case of Dr. WG Grace, the great batsman of England from 1882 to 1905, such considerations were not raised. When Grace was getting his runs and centuries there was neither the ICC nor did England have a central cricket control body. Why were WG Grace's matches considered official Test matches?

So, my contention is that if Grace is acknowledged as an official Test cricketer and all his performance recognized, then why not in Deodhar's case? Yes, while there is every reason to recognize the great feats of WG Grace but at the same time it is our paramount duty to acknowledge the feats of DB Deodhar as well by way of natural justice. How can there be two different sets of rules for two people?

Deodhar's status is on much firmer grounds than WG's. In Deodhar's time the ICC was already in existence (1909). Deodhar played for a representative team of Indians from all over the country. In WG's case it was not so. At the time it was the prerogative of the host county to decide on the composition of the England XI. Thus, the England teams were not representative teams, but a selection based on the whims and fancies of the county hoisting the match.

As mentioned earlier a prime example of the trend of the time is the omission of Kumar Shri Ranjitsinhji from the Lord's Test in 1896 and his debut in the next Test match at Manchester followed by the one at Oval.

At that point of time Ranjitsinhji was the most prolific scorer in England. There could be no reason not to select him in a properly and fairly selected England team. But the powers-that-be at Lord's did not want him in the England side. They were not national selectors but men who would arbitrarily decide on who would play on their own ground.

Similarly, the men in administration at Manchester and Oval had their own minds. They too were not national selectors but simply men who loved to take their own decisions about the composition of the England XI playing on their ground. These men at Manchester and Oval decided that they would have Ranji in the England XI. And that's exactly what they did. Thus, Grace and Ranji were not chosen by any representative bodies, whereas Deodhar was. Yet, Grace and Ranji are considered to be official Test players and ironically Deodhar is not.

ICC must take the initiative of pragmatic thinking. There has to be consistency of approach. If ICC insists upon centralized bodies selecting representative teams in the case of West Indies, New Zealand and the sub-continental countries then the same logic should hold good for England, Australia and South Africa. How can there be different yardsticks for different countries to attain the same status?

Today, ICC is no longer the monopoly of the white races. There are representatives from all participating nations. Some very eminent cricketing names are heading the top committees. Hence there is every reason for cricket lovers to feel that that there should be logical handling of affairs at the highest level. Why should prominent people at the ICC allow disparities to continue? Why should able administrators toe the line of arbitrary thinking? Why should the cricket experts of ICC parrot the mistakes committed earlier?

Some people tend to argue that the past should not be raked up: the mistakes of the past should be allowed to continue as a matter of convention. This idea has no justification whatsoever. If in the 21st century we cannot think in terms of logic and reasoning, then how would progressive thinking take place? At present in every field of endeavour, the shortcomings of the past are being corrected and replaced by new discoveries, modern ideas and, most importantly, by logical reasoning. Why should cricket be an unfortunate exception?

Cricket has come a long way from the days of under-arm bowling and two-stump wickets. Modern innovations have introduced new forms of cricket: the equipment and the techniques have altered, the strategies are different, the dress code has little link with the past, even the cricketing lexicon has undergone great changes. The whole cricketing movement is evolving in a manner no one would have dared to predict even 3 decades ago. In such a scenario why should the history of cricket not be judged from the altar of pragmatism? Why should we accept the mistakes of the past to cloud our judgement?

Forgotten Heroes

The Immortal Unheralded Trio: Pavri, Baloo and Deodhar

If the triumvirate in the Hindu pantheon is Brahma, Vishnu and Maheshwar, then the trio in the Indian cricketing pantheon would be Mehallasha Pavri (1866–1946), Baloo Palvankar (1875–1955) and Dinkar Balwant Deodhar (1892–1993). They were destined to lay down the foundation of the Golden Age of Indian cricket.

Each of them was a man of impeccable credentials. They complemented just as they contrasted each other. All three were magnificent cricketers. Pavri was a fast-medium bowler; Baloo an orthodox left-arm spin bowler and Deodhar a batsman of rare vintage. They were the real pioneers who not only built the foundation of Indian cricket but also paved the path for the future generations to thrive and prosper. They carried the zeal of the crusaders as well as the faith of the pilgrims. In the face of diverse adversities, these marvellous men showed the world that the Indians were as brilliant as any other in the world.

Mehallasha Pavri

They contrasted each other just as well. Pavri, hailing from a wealthy Parsee background, was a very successful doctor by profession. Baloo, born into a *harijan* family of social outcastes,

Dinkar Balwant Deodhar

was a poverty-stricken groundsman. And Deodhar, a professor of Sanskrit, came from an educated, middle-class background.

The high noon of their careers too did not quite coincide. It spanned a generation beginning from the mid-1890s to the 1930s. One emerged as the other made way. Pavri left serious cricket around 1910 as Baloo continued. Deodhar's emerged as Baloo dominated between 1911 and 1920. Then Deodhar took over and carried on, incredibly, till the late 1940s. But he was at his best in the 1920s and 1930s. In modern lexicon they would be known as The Generation First.

It is indeed ironical that the three men, who contributed the most to India's emergence as a Test-playing nation in 1932, were never to play official Tests for their beloved motherland. Their destiny too was common: to pave the path for posterity. They were men of dignity and discipline; of character and camaraderie; of valour and vision. They did not know the art of compromise and consequently suffered deprivations and neglect, particularly Baloo and Deodhar.

These glorious men revived the game of cricket in India. They were our cricketing forefathers in the Golden Age of Indian cricket. Their natural athleticism, their positive approach, their courage and determination and their exceptional skills made it easier for us to believe that that the game did exist in this land of ours millenniums ago.

Mehallasha Edulji Pavri was a product of the Parsee community in the latter half of the 19th century. Born at Navsari in Gujarat in 1866, he was drawn into the vortex of cricket in Bombay at a time when the mercantile Parsee community was more than eager to befriend the British rulers. The Parsees realized that cricket was the ideal vehicle to gain easy access to the British. Learning the rudiments of the game by watching the Britons at the Bombay *maidans*, the Parsees decided that they too would have their own club teams and play against the white men on equal terms.

It was easier said than done. The Britons in India did play against the Parsees, but they were sarcastic, condescending and downright insulting at times. The affronts made the Parsees more determined than ever. They made up their minds to learn the game as fast as possible.

Even as early as 1886 a Parsee cricket team set sail for England to enable the players to adapt themselves to the varying conditions and pitches. Only the elder cricketers of the community, who could afford to pay the passage fare and the tour cost, went. As was to be expected, the Parsee team fared disastrously against the English teams, who were far more experienced and superior in every department of the game. The young Pavri was not in the 1st Parsee team to go to England.

But by the time the next Parsee team was selected to tour England in 1988, Pavri was an automatic choice. The big-built fast medium bowler had been performing magnificently in the inter-club matches as well as in the limited opportunities against teams comprising expatriate Britons.

On English wickets, Pavri was a man inspired. He unleashed his thunderbolts with nagging accuracy. Stumps went cart-wheeling with welcome regularity. A natural athlete, he kept his ears and eyes open as he picked up the finer skills from the masters of seam and swing, especially the England Test bowler, Lockwood. He added the break-back to his repertoire and felt equally at ease with the old ball as with the new.

By dint of Pavri's personal success, the profile of his team improved by leaps. Whereas in 1886 the Parsees won just one match, losing 19 out of 28; this time the equation read: 8 victories and 11 defeats out of 31 matches. Surely, a remarkable progress by any yardstick.

For Pavri, the tour of England was a revelation. In India the expatriate Britons had scoffed at the cricketing efforts of the Parsees, but in England the Britons were genuinely generous with their praise and guidance. Pavri's extraordinary performance of 170 wickets at only 11.66 earned respect and plaudits.

In a particular encounter with the Gentlemen of England at Eastbourne in Sussex, the Parsees were forced to follow-on. On the second attempt they left the opponents with just 120 runs to win. The strong English team was no doubt extremely confident, but the spirited Pavri had other ideas. His whip-lash action bundled the opposition for only 56 runs and he, the prime architect, captured 6 wickets. This was the match that heralded the rise of the magnificent fast-medium bowler, the embryo from which Kapil Dev was to flower in the following century.

In 1890 Vernon's team arrived in India and in 1892 it was the turn of Lord Hawke's team. Against both the sides, Pavri's domination was so very overwhelming that he was invited to play in the county championship in England for Middlesex in 1896. Thus, Pavri becomes the first India-bred cricketer to have played in the county championship in England. Ranjitsinhji too made his county championship debut in 1896 for Sussex but he is not included in this category as he learnt and played basically in England. Ranji however had got his Cambridge Blue in1893.

Pavri played in the communal tournaments in India, which went under the nomenclature of Presidency matches and the Triangular tournament, till 1912. After that he was totally immersed in his medical profession. As befitted his profession, he was a rare deity in the pantheon of Indian cricket. His deeds heralded to the world that the Indians could learn the game on their own and be as good as any in the world of men.

Pavri died in Bombay in 1946. He authored an excellent book titled *'Parsi Cricket'* where he very meticulously recorded some very interesting statistics and illuminating revelations about the early years of cricket in India. He was most certainly the chief architect who brought Indian cricket into the focus of the British population in India. It was Pavri's prolific performance at cricket that influenced the expatriate Britons to start the Presidency matches thereby heralding the beginning of first-class cricket matches in the sub-continent in 1894.

✶ ✶ ✶ ✶ ✶ ✶

The first India-born and bred cricketer of international eminence was not a maharaja. Nor did he belong to the elites among the Parsees, Hindus, Muslims, Sikhs or Christians, who patronized and dominated Indian cricket in the early stages. The first genuine international class Indian cricketer was a *chamaar*, a social outcaste. His name was Baloo Palvankar and he hailed from an obscure corner of Maharashtra.

Baloo was born in1875 at Dharwad, but soon his father migrated to Poona where he got a job in the army factory. Extremely poor, the family had meagre resources of sustenance. The young Baloo had little option but to leave school early in life to augment the family income. His first job was with a Parsee cricket club where he rolled and swept the ground.

By 1892 however he got employment in the exclusive environment of Poona Gymkhana, where he was required to assist the chief groundsman. Humiliation and hunger, deprivation and uncertainty were his constant companions.

Baloo was a most unlikely champion. He had neither wealth nor lineage to support him in any sphere of life. His daily existence was one of struggle. However, he paid minute attention as the British cricketers practised on the lawns of Poona Gymkhana, an exclusive European

Baloo Palvankar

preserve at the time. He watched and absorbed their mannerisms, their styles, their techniques and their attitudes.

One day with not a single bowler available, the star batter of the European team 'Junglee' Greig ordered Baloo to bowl at him at the nets. Baloo picked up the ball, rolled back his shirt sleeves and went left-arm round-the-wicket to the accomplished batsman. Greig was confounded by the deceptive curl as the spinning ball swerved in and then spun out. Instantly Greig realized the talent latent in the young man. From the next day, Greig would come early and induce Baloo to bowl at him for hours. Thus, began Baloo's tryst with destiny.

Word soon spread that the young *harijan*-groundsman possessed exceptional bowling skills. But the conservative, high-caste Hindus of Poona would not even contemplate giving him a trial, far less selecting him in the Hindu club teams. In the caste-ridden ambience of Poona at the time, the low-born *chamaar* had little sympathy and less opportunity. Fortunately, around this time Baloo's father went to Bombay, where the cosmopolitan clime afforded him comparatively a little easier social mobility.

Here too, at the Hindu Gymkhana the orthodox elements were initially not in favour of playing with a "low-born" *harijan*. But then regular defeats at the hands of the European and Parsee oppositions compelled them to include Baloo in their team. Using all his skills he was an immediate success in the local matches, which made him an automatic choice for the Hindu team in the triangular tournament where the Hindus competed with the Parsees and the European expatriates. Almost overnight, as it were, the Hindus began to win matches and titles. The primary reason was the fantastic exploits of the social pariah, the outcaste Baloo.

From 1907 to 1920 he was the best bowler in the land, Hindu or otherwise. Man of phenomenal performance and remarkable consistency. Even though he was winning them trophies, the Hindus did not allow him to sit beside them to have his cricket lunches! Despite opposition from his own community to his leadership, late in life Baloo had the satisfaction to lead the Hindus to victory in the Quadrangular of 1920. This was most certainly a rare achievement. For a "low-caste" Hindu to give leadership to the supposed higher castes was indeed a major breakthrough in the social fabric of the Hindu community at the time.

For the sake of self-interest and convenience, the "upper-class" Hindus accepted a social outcaste to play alongside them. The man, who was judged to be an untouchable because of his birth, now became a hero because of his genius. This was the hypocrisy of the ruling classes.

In mythology too, a similar comparison would be found. In the Mahabharata. Krishna, the Jadav warrior-prince, hailed not from Aryan lineage but from a non-Aryan tribal background. The non-Aryan tribal people were not considered at par with the Aryan ruling classes. Yet when Krishna's great qualities of wisdom, intelligence, skills and marksmanship came into limelight, the Aryan community immediately accepted him as one of their own by changing his nomenclature to *Bratya-Aryan*.

In 1911 when the Maharaja of Patiala decided to take an all-India cricket

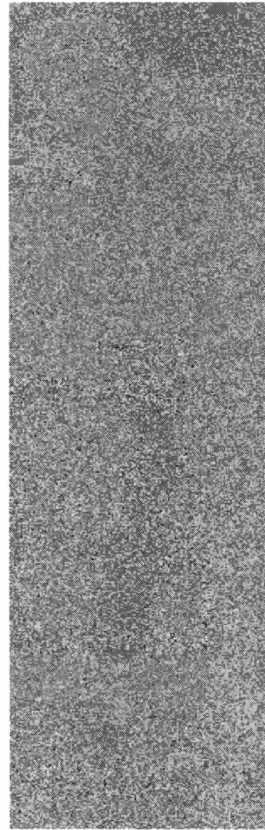

Rev. John Glennie Greig (1871–1958): Nicknamed 'Junglee', he discovered and highlighted the world-class prowess of Baloo thus doing an exceptional service to Indian society and Indian cricket. Outstanding batsman for the Europeans and Hampshire. Highly respected Roman Catholic priest. Honoured by Britain for services to the Empire. An impeccable specimen of humanity: sadly, totally forgotten

team to England, Baloo was an automatic choice. At the time he was not only the best left-arm spinner in the land, he was also a very effective batsman in the middle order.

In England, Baloo created havoc match after match. He did not worry about the cold, blistery weather. Nor did he find any time to bother about the ever-changing conditions and the varying pitches on which he had no experience earlier. He hardly got any help by way of guidance from his fellow players. And on the field the support from his fieldsmen was almost negligible. The social pariah made no discrimination in his opponents as he teased and tormented royalty, commoners, university dons and professionals at will with the skills of his magical fingers.

He exhibited to the Britons as well as to his fellow 'upper-class' Indians what a social outcaste from an obscure village in India was capable of, if given the right opportunities. It is to the credit of the liberated section of the Britons to hail him as at par with the best of left-arm spinners of the world at the time. Thus, the deprived and discriminated Indian *chamaar* showed the world that skill and merit were not the exclusive preserve of any particular section of society. Unfortunately, even today the lesson of Baloo Palvankar has hardly seeped into the mind of the Indian caste-ridden society.

Baloo made the world realize that the Indians, who were forced to occupy the lowest rung of the social ladder, were in no way inferior to any other Indian nor to anyone in the world. Later Baloo was joined in the Hindu team by his three brothers – Shivram, Vithal and Ganpat – each a brilliant performer in his own right.

Comparatively, they might have suffered marginally less than what Baloo had to face, to establish themselves as cricketers, but their life story was as much of humiliation and discrimination as Baloo's was. These four brothers made the Hindu team the best in the land. By dint of character and capability, they paved the path for India's entry into international cricket but they themselves were never a part of it, as their best days had ended before India began to play Test cricket. Height of irony, indeed.

Unfortunately, the caste Hindus never treated the Palvankar brothers well; certainly, never as social equals. They were discriminated against on and off the field. They were forced to have their cricket lunch away from the tables of the caste Hindus. They were made to feel small in various ways. Men far more inferior to them in merit were given favours because of their supposed 'class' and 'caste'.

The hypocrisy of Indian social life was laid bare on the cricket fields of the sub-continent. The Palvankar siblings were tolerated only because of their ability to enable the Hindus to win victories. It was a shameless case of exploitation on the part of the Hindu community.

Although Baloo received no formal schooling, he was far more educated, in the real sense of the word, than the caste Hindus who had the advantage of attending prominent schools and universities. He had impeccable manners, a cultured voice and a liberal attitude. He was a man of great dignity. Despite being at the receiving end of the worst forms of humiliation imaginable, not once did Baloo behave in a manner that could be faulted. His general demeanour was of a cultured and dignified man.

On his triumphant return from England in 1911, the prominent social activists like Gokhale, Ranade and Tilak hailed his greatness in public announcements. Even Bhimrao Ambedkar, then a young student, became a self-confessed ardent fan of his.

Although he was far superior to any of his cricket contemporaries in India, and he was among the best left-arm spinner of the world in his time, cricket ultimately denied him the minimum of recognition. In death, as in life, he was never to receive his due acknowledgement. His was a story of exploitation. Mercilessly humiliated as was the norm for people belonging to his caste, even his great cricketing credentials did not earn him any benefit.

Whatever he got from cricket was not for his own benefit but for the benefit of the upper-class Hindus. He and his brothers were merely pawns to be exploited and forgotten, totally at the mercy of caste-ridden Hindus. Baloo however overcame the odds in his own inimitable manner. He even led the Hindu team to victory in the 1920 Quadrangular tournament.

With the advent of Mohandas Gandhi and his advocacy in favour of the *harijans*, the prospects of the 'untouchables' showed the scantiest of improvement. This marginal change of attitude resulted in the Hindu Mahasabha persuading Baloo to contest a seat in the election to the Bombay Municipality in the 1930s. According to renowned historian Ramchandra Guha "... Baloo Palvankar's decision to stand for the election seems to have been a "world's first" as far as a professional cricketer was concerned..." For the record, Baloo narrowly lost the contest but then he did not make the slightest of effort to capitalize on his high status as a sportsman.

For that matter, nor did Baloo change his religious belief to Buddhism in response to a call from his friend and fan, Ambedkar, who was convinced that the 'untouchables' had no future within the Hindu community and so he wanted all his fellow 'untouchables' to convert themselves into Buddhists.

Baloo did not change his religion as he felt that with Mahatma Gandhi's emergence and influence the status of his community would improve and that they would become an important part of the mainstream.

The contradiction in approach between the two friends drew them apart. In 1937, despite reluctance on his part, Baloo was coerced to fight an election against the formidable Dr. Ambedkar and, as apprehended, lost the contest. Since then, once again he went back to obscurity and no one came to his help in later life.

No selection or coaching assignments awaited him although players far inferior were holding such elevated posts. If only Baloo had forsaken Hinduism and embraced Buddhism, he would surely have been a well-known name in political and sports circles. He died in 1955 in penury, thoroughly forgotten by the very men he had helped to prosper. Every Indian cricketer owes him an eternal debt. He is the first ever Indian cricketer who heralded the superiority of Indian cricketers to the world at large. He is the man who opened the door for the modern cricketer to earn respect abroad.

Here is a man who has been forgotten by historians, both sports and political. His only fault was that he was born on the wrong side of the fence. Cricket forgot his superiority status. Politics forgot his minority status. Cricket historians forgot him because India did not play Test cricket in his heydays. Political historians forgot him because he had fallen away from his one-time friend, Bhimrao Ambedkar.

No national award, no national recognition, no financial benefit was ever granted to this dignified genius. Not that he cared for any. He left behind the memory of a legend that should make every Indian cricket lover feel guilty of having forsaken him.

The former English cricketer and author E.H.D. Sewell has very appropriately written "...Baloo is a bowler most of our county teams would be very glad to have him in their XI..." Baloo, the social-outcaste, belonged to the aristocratic class of left-arm spinners. He was the pioneering genius, who lit the paths of the Mankads, the Duranis and the Bedis.

* * * * * *

Dinkar Balwant Deodhar was born in Pune in 1892 and from an early age was exposed to the legendary exploits of Shivaji Chhatrapati. A staunch Hindu of impeccable credentials, to Deodhar cricket meant merely another route to attainment of salvation.

If Pavri and Baloo, primarily by their exploits on tours to England, had fired the imagination of youth in those hoary days, it was left to Deodhar to give the Indians the taste of success first-hand. For the first time ever, a representative team of the colonial masters was subjugated by an Indian on Indian soil in full view of his countrymen. It appeared that Deodhar's mission was to prove to the ruling Britons that the Indian subjects were capable of surpassing their best players at their own game.

If any single Indian player can claim to have taken the country to official Test match status, it was most certainly the erudite Sanskrit scholar from Pune. On a winter morning in 1926, the grassy Bombay Gymkhana pitch laden with fresh due beckoned the great fast-medium bowler Maurice Tate to exhibit his mastery as the India team faced the daunting task of facing Arthur Gilligan's England (then MCC) team. This was the occasion for which the 34-year old Sanskrit pundit was waiting for years.

Dinkar Balwant Deodhar

Combining doggedness with exemplary strokes, Deodhar relentlessly went on and on. The imposing MCC total of 362 was passed and only then did Deodhar allow his stupendous concentration to flag. He contributed a masterly 148 out of the team's total of 437, a distinct lead of 75 runs over an England team comprising prominent Test cricketers.

No longer would the Englishmen make fun of Indian cricketers; no longer would there be sniggers; no longer would anyone dare to take the Indians lightly. That day he was not only batting for his team, he was writing the script of self-respect of a people subjugated to indignities and worse. His innings would have made Kautilya proud.

MCC skipper Arthur Gilligan, gentleman to the core, was enchanted by Deodhar's innings of character and skill. Gilligan went back to England and took personal initiative to propose that India deserved to be among the nations playing official Test matches. Thus, India came to join the Imperial Cricket Conference (now, International Cricket Council or ICC) as an official Test team and made her debut in 1932 against England at the Lord's.

But such is the irony of this game that the man, who was primarily responsible to elevate India to official Test match status, never got a single opportunity to play Test cricket himself. When India went on her inaugural Test tour of England in 1932, the name of Deodhar was missing. An act of sacrilege, if ever there was one. By 1932 the cricket crusaders had given way to cricket conspirators. The new breed of administrators publicised that Deodhar at 40 was too old to play for the country.

Yes, at 40 a cricketer may have been thought to be old by conventional standards. But Deodhar was not a man to conform to stereotype patterns. He was actually physically fitter than most not only in 1932 but also in 1936 when the second India team went to England. At that time, he was a regular player for the Hindu team in the Quadrangular and Pentangular as well as for Maharashtra in the Ranji Trophy. His prolific performance in the first-class cricket in the 1930s was far superior to most of the men who played for India at the time.

Deodhar actually was a victim of conspiracy. This educated man was a free-thinking, liberated soul. He never formed groups. His individual streak and love for his own province forbade him from joining the service of the influential maharajas. Thus, his erudition and upright character became a noose around his neck.

The outspoken professor blamed C.K. Nayudu for his omission from the 1932 team to England. Deodhar felt that Nayudu never wanted him around as then Nayudu's influence would wane. This attitude of self-interest by the principal players has always dominated Indian cricket and consequently the national team has suffered over the years.

However, it is to Deodhar's credit that he took his fate in his firm strides. He played for Maharashtra till the age of 54! Even at that age he was prolific in his batting performance. At the age of 48, he scored 246 against Bombay and ultimately led his team to victory over Madras in the Ranji Trophy final.

As if this was not unique enough, he scored a century in each innings against Nawanagar at the age of 52! Such is the irony of destiny. That a man who was eminently successful in his endeavours, had to remain a silent spectator because of the conspiracy and intrigues of his own countrymen.

After retiring from the game, Deodhar was a very responsible national selector. Here too he left his imprint. He did not allow Anthony D'Mello, the Board President at the time, any favours. He was firmly opposed to D'Mello for trying to meddle in the selection of the national team. For this courageous approach of his, Deodhar suffered but then he could not be enticed to compromise with his principles. He was responsible for the rise of some of our genuine world-class players like Vinoo Mankad and Vijay Hazare.

For a man's of Deodhar's deep erudition and strong character, it was not the result but the effort that mattered. Rarely, if ever, we have seen such a *karma-yogi* on the cricket ground.

Every Indian cricketer, of whatever hue, owes an eternal gratitude to these magnificent pioneers. They laid the path and paved the way so that others could have a smooth passage. Let us not forget these immortal souls. Our very existence as cricketers and cricket lovers is because of their supreme sacrifices.

I met Prof Deodhar just once. Way back during the Indian cricket season of 1972–73. Bengal had just been beaten by Maharashtra in a Ranji Trophy quarter-final tie at Pune. That was our skipper Chuni Goswami's farewell match for Bengal and the last match of my debut season.

Inside the pavilion sat an elderly man with eyes glued to the match. Chunida asked me, "You always keep blabbering about cricket. Can you identify the gentleman sitting on the cane chair?"

I had a good look and asked, "Will he be Prof Deodhar?"

"Good. Then come I will introduce you to him."

"But does he know you?" I asked.

Chunida smiled and gave a sidelong glance, "Everybody in India knows me."

As we went near the man, the elderly gentleman looked at Chunida and said, "Chuni, happy to see that you are still playing." Chunida nodded and shook hands with him.

The moment Chunida introduced me, the man said, "Good technique and temperament, but poor physique. Will never play for India."

I was stunned by his assessment. Had a very successful debut season and played a fairly responsible innings in this match too. Yet the gentleman was so very discouraging. But, to be honest, he was dead correct. My physique was never strong enough. Suffered from a congenital heart ailment.

Immediately I said, "Sir, I do not crave to be a Test player. I want to be like you."

"What do you mean? Like me, in which way?"

"Sir, I want to be an academic first and only then a cricketer."

The elderly gentleman smiled and grasped my hand, "That's the spirit I like."That grasp was not the limp handshake of an 80-year-old man. It was the Maratha grip that finished Afzal Khan. Full of steel and rock.

The conversation with the living legend was enlightening. I did not want to let him go. He also seemed to enjoy my company. When I asked him about his cricket career, he merely said, "It is for others to judge. I was happy to have kept my backbone straight throughout."

I quipped, "Sir, your protégés have answered on your behalf." Furrowed his eyebrows and nodded.

"Sir, please consider me to be your Ekalavya."

Did I see the suggestion of a strange smile cross his face? Did not say anything beyond, "In that case you will lose a lot." When I touched his feet, he was visibly touched. Just said, "If you remain straight, God will always be with you."

He got up and strode out. He was 80 plus at the time. Sturdy and strong. No support. Not even a walking stick. Every inch a philosopher-warrior. I had met my boyhood idol Chhatrapati Shivaji. I had met my Dronacharya. The silhouette left, leaving behind an ever-lasting impression. He left just as he had spent his life. In splendid isolation.

Among the great architects who laid the foundation of Indian cricket: from left – Vijay Merchant, CK Nayudu and DB Deodhar

Ambassadors

Vijay Hazare (1915–2004)

Was Vijay Hazare a victim of apartheid or some other discrimination in Indian cricket? Vijay Samuel Hazare was a Christian and so could not take part in the Quadrangular cricket championship in the 1930s as only the Europeans, Hindus, Parsees and Muslims were eligible. However, the Sikhs were considered in the Hindu team. This victimization must have rankled in the young man's mind because when he got the opportunity he sent his oppressors scurrying for cover.

Vijay Hazare

Vijay Hazare came to the forefront of national cricket in 1938 when the Pentangular cricket championship replaced the Quadrangular with the 'Rest' side taking part as the fifth team, alongside the Europeans, the Parsees, the Hindus and the Muslims.

Immediately, he put everyone in the shade, even Vijay Merchant, then a premier batsman of the world. Hazare's prodigious feats in the few years of Pentangular cricket read: 1 triple hundred, 1 double hundred, 2 centuries and 4 fifties in only 14 innings with an average of 101 and an aggregate of 1212 runs.

After making his first-class debut in 1936 for Maharashtra, Hazare lost the prime of his cricket life to the World War II. Born at Sangli in Maharashtra in 1915, Vijay Hazare could make his official Test debut only at the matured age of 31, when he went to England with Iftikar Ali Khan Pataudi's team in 1946.

Despite the very late start to his Test cricket career, Hazare exhibited to the world that he was not to be trifled with. In 1947–48, he went to Australia with Lala Amarnath's team and was an outstanding success. Ray Lindwall and Keith Miller, the foremost and fearsome pace duo in Don Bradman's arsenal, held no terrors for him. Far from being bogged down against the best team in the world, Hazare alerted the cricket world with centuries in either innings at Adelaide.

No one else had ever treated Bradman's team, reputedly the best-ever in international cricket, with such disdain. He was the first among Indians to have scored a century in each innings of a Test match. Not against any namby-pamby team but against the best

Vijay Hazare, Sir Don Bradman and skipper Lala Amarnath during India's tour to Australia in 1947–48

team in the world at the time and on their backyard. It appeared that he was giving a fitting reply to all those who had conspired to keep his guru, Deodhar, out of the India team in the 1930s.

The man was nothing less than a marvel. Probably the greatest batsman India has produced. He played the fearsome pace of Ray Lindwall, Keith Miller and Fred Trueman without even thigh pads. The helmet and chest-guard would surely have been a self-inflicted insult. He played the swing and cut of Alec Bedser and Fazal Mahmood with rare composure. But most important, he played on uncovered pitches, where the batsman was exposed to the vagaries of nature.

This is one aspect of cricket that is strangely forgotten when cricket followers start comparing the past greats with the modern masters.

This issue of playing on moisture laden wickets day in, day out required the best of technique just to survive. To master such conditions, one had to be a rare breed indeed. It was under such trying conditions that Vijay Hazare not only survived but prospered.

He did not have the benefit of any influential lobby of Indian cricket. He was always his own man. A genuine protégé of Dinkar Balwant Deodhar. A man who stood head and shoulders above all his contemporaries by sheer weight of performance. His run-scoring ability and his consistency have hardly ever been matched, earlier or later. Twice he scored triple centuries in first-class cricket.

One of those was a gem of 316 for Maharashtra against Baroda in 1939–40, which happened to be his first century in Ranji Trophy. The other triple century, 309 out of a total of 387, was against the Hindus in the Pentangular Final on 1943, which happens to be the highest score in the communal tournaments of the time. The domination was such that while Hazare scored a triple century, from the other end just 78 runs were scored!

This innings proved that Hazare had the ability to tear an attack apart in answer to those who said that he could not decimate the opposition. Was it done in revenge for not being allowed to play in the Quadrangular? Hazare, a man of very few words, had no time for verbal duels. He preferred to silence his detractors through the broad bat of his.

As if this was not enough, Hazare saw to it that his name was forever sculpted in the annals of world cricket records. In 1946, with Gul Mohammed, he amassed 577 runs for the 4th wicket against CK Nayudu's Holkar in the Ranji Trophy final of 1946–47. This partnership of 577 remained the highest-ever partnership for any wicket till 2006. Still remains the highest 4th wicket record in world cricket. This is one world record that has stayed on for decades and might remain that way for all time to come. This would indeed be a fitting tribute to a man who has never received the recognition that was his rightful due.

It is very conveniently forgotten that Vijay Hazare was the first captain to lead India to a Test match victory. For all their abilities as leaders, neither CK Nayudu nor Lala Amarnath could achieve this significant mark. Hazare's young lieutenants saw to it that England (then MCC) was defeated at Chepauk in 1951–52 to give India her first victory in her 25th Test match. In that match, Pankaj Roy and Polly Umrigar did their captain and country proud with centuries. The ever-green all-rounder Vinoo Mankad was the chief architect of the famous innings victory with 12 wickets.

Following year, Hazare was leading India in England. The murky environment had the Indians in no end of trouble. But in those gloomy forebodings, one man – Vijay Hazare – stood out along with his protégé Vijay Manjrekar. In the 1st Test at Leeds with Bedser and Trueman on the rampage, India lost 3 wickets for 42 before Hazare (89) and Vijay Manjrekar (133) stood ground to build a partnership of 222 runs. In the second innings as India lay in shambles with 4 wickets down for 0 runs, again it was the reassuring stocky figure of the captain who shouldered the crisis with a stolid 56. Such acts were frequent with Hazare but were never highlighted in the annals of Indian cricket history.

Vijay Hazare enjoyed a very good rapport with the cricket connoisseurs all over the country. Eden Gardens seemed to be his particular favourite, where he rarely failed. After his Eden Gardens exploits along with his dear friends Hemu Adhikari and Dattu Phadkar, he would be welcomed at the Samarth home on Lake Road for his favourite *shrikhand*.

In those days Test matches were hardly played on a regular basis. However, Test players arrived in India with combined teams (far stronger than some contemporary Test sides) to play Tests which were regarded as unofficial Tests. These strong, combined sides were known as Commonwealth teams

These teams had men of the calibre of Frank Worrell, George Tribe, Bruce Dooland, Jack Livingstone and others of international repute. Against such strong teams, Hazare made it a habit of scoring highly and consistently. At Eden Gardens, twice he met the Commonwealth teams, and, on both occasions, he collected his usual quota of 100 plus runs.

He was indeed a phenomenon. No pitch bothered him. No condition upset him. No opposition scared him. While at the crease he was in a cocoon of his own without a care in the world. It was said that his concentration was such that while he batted he would not even speak to his batting partner!

Vijay Samuel Hazare did not enjoy the luxury of injuries and lack of form. He was a warrior first and remained a warrior till the end in the mould of his master, Deodhar. Vijay Hazare would fight for the honour of his country till the last drop of his blood. He did not bother about batting positions. In fact, weak oppositions had better chances of getting him out. He would have been dismissed out of sheer mercy and boredom.

While Hazare is praised for his batting prowess, there is a tendency to forget his bowling potential. He thrived on dual responsibilities. He had an unusual action. Rather than bowling over-arm, he had a very prominent side-arm or round-arm action, almost similar to the Sri Lankan Lasith Malinga. But that did not stop his out-swingers and off-cutters from getting 599 scalps in first-class cricket and 20 victims in Test matches. In only 30 Tests over a span of 7 years, he scored 2192 runs at a most impressive average of 47.65 with 7 centuries. In first class matches he scored 18,754 runs at 58.06 with 60 centuries.

The great batsman was a great human being, too. Self-effacing modesty was his hallmark. He was a generous man who influenced a whole generation of top-class cricketers, including Chandu Borde. The short, strong man strode like a colossus but with the feet firmly on the ground. Like his guru, Deodhar, the immortal Vijay Hazare was close to the soil and close to the young players around him.

He was the role model of the 50s, 60s and 70s generations. At a time when cricketers continue to get chances despite repeated failures, Hazare's career was cut short after just one unsuccessful series in West Indies. I suspect he failed because he never really had the urge to thrive against weak oppositions. Similar to Gundappa Vishwanath, he was back-stabbed by the very people he had helped to prosper.

Extremely quiet he was on and off the field. He would guide only when asked. Never on his own. He would never impose his will on others. The young players of Maharashtra and Baroda found in him an inspiring role-model. Because he taught not by words but by action.

Vijay Hazare's nephew, the prominent first-class cricketer and excellent umpire Sanjay Hazare recollected, "Uncle was a strong-silent person. If forced, he would not talk about his own exploits but would always keep praising others. He would never answer back any silly criticism made against him." Straight to the point was Sanjay, my friend: the same blood as Vijay Hazare's. Vijay Hazare would not waste time and effort with verbal duels: a great lesson for most of us.

It is to the credit of Board of Control for Cricket in India (BCCI) that they have immortalized his name through the Vijay Hazare Trophy. When the grand gentleman breathed his last in 2004, he at least had the satisfaction to know that Indian cricket had not forgotten him.

But another issue: do the modern players, who take part in the Vijay Hazare Trophy matches, know who the person was? Spoke to some and was surprised to find that they had very scanty knowledge and were least keen to know more! That is one side of the real picture of Indian cricket today.

Vijay Hazare with his wife and nephew, Sanjay Hazare

Kapil Dev (1959–)

First saw him at a Ranji Trophy encounter at Eden in 1975 perhaps, when he was in his teens. The lanky fast bowler was all energy and aggression. On a dew-laden, uncovered, green pitch he had Bengal down to 0 for 2 in his first over and then two more followed. A reasonable partnership between PC Poddar and the present writer helped Bengal to a respectable total.

Ultimately Bengal won the match against a very young, inexperienced Haryana team who found it difficult to adjust to the seaming conditions. But the lasting image of the match was the advent of an exceptional

Kapil Dev

fast bowler. A rarity in Indian cricket in the mid-1970s. Haryana's Rajinder Goel and Ravinder Chadha concurred with me that a unique talent was among us.

We were not wrong. Within a year or two, Bengal was at Haryana's den at Rai for a Ranji Trophy tie. This time the pitch was a paradise for spinners. Full of dry, loose dust, where the uneven bounce made a mockery of a cricket pitch. But the main issue was that even on that pitch, the young fast bowler was at his fearsome best.

He did not bother about conditions. He aimed at the stumps every delivery as he had done at Eden Gardens. Amazing control. He could

swing and seam as he intended. Never quite worried about conditions, situations, oppositions. He was confident of his own ability. With his impressive arsenal laid bare, he impressed the national selector present at the ground, Jayasinghrao Ghorpade, and was in the India team within months.

Came back to Calcutta again in 1979–80 to haunt Bengal at Eden. Now he was among the premier all-rounders of the world having just reached 1000 runs and 100 wickets in record time. So popular was he at Calcutta that the thousands who came to watch the match cheered more for Kapil's Haryana than for the home team!

Despite conceding the first innings lead, we scripted a victory against the likes of a very strong Haryana team boasting Kapil Dev and Rajinder Goel in the XI. After the match Kapil came to our dressing room, shook my hands in congratulations and smiled, "I wish you got the single to reach your century, but we won the match." The gesture, the honesty, the innocence was not lost on all those who witnessed the scene.

Child is the prophecy of man. So uttered Mark Twain. The prophetic words describe the man who erased the myth for ever that an Indian pace bowler can never put the fear of devil in opposing batsmen. Kapil Dev, more than any other Indian cricketer, really did shake up the world as he thundered in. Whether to bowl or to bat. His approach was the approach of the hurricane. He was always on the fast lane. Wreaked havoc; fast and fearsome.

Never did anything by halves. If a ball was to be hit, he would give it a real blow. If the issue was bowling fast, he would go full tilt at the batter's throat. No half measures for this daring soul. This was certainly not the conventional Indian attitude. Was his emergence as a fast bowler an aberration?

It could well have been. Never before did we see an Indian bowler trying to get a batsman out by sheer pace. Mohammed Nissar in the 1930s and Ramakant Desai in the early 1960s were the rare exceptions but then they bowled on Indian wickets which were not the feather-beds of the 1980s and 1990s. When Kapil came into prominence in the mid-1970s the Indian pitches had acquired a reputation for being over-friendly to spinners. From the 1980s those were absolutely 'sleeping beauties' on which even below average batsmen moved around with inflated egos.

In such conditions, generally no fast bowler would even dream of trying to extract pace and bounce from the pitch. But the young lad from Chandigarh put all those conventional theories into the dust-bin. No cobweb cluttered his innocent mind. He wanted to bowl fast and that was it.

One particular incident cemented his resolve. Once at a junior cricket camp under BCCI he had asked for some extra *rotis*. The official supervisor, a former Test cricketer chided him by saying, "What for? What do you do?" Young Kapil had replied," I am a fast bowler." The supervisor laughed, "Fast bowler? In India no one can bowl fast." This was the insult that had the young Kapil all fired up to prove his detractors wrong.

Kapil has done many exceptional exploits over the years. He is the first player from a small town to have stayed back at home in Chandigarh instead of going over to the more influential metropolitan cities like Delhi, Chennai, Kolkata and Mumbai. Talented young Indian cricketers would normally leave their hearth in small towns and rural areas to seek fame and fortune in major cities.

Kapil Dev with Gulu Ezekiel, an eminent sports analyst and journalist. Gulu has contributed to more than 150 publications in India and around the world

But the fact remains that Kapil Dev did not seek any gain from anywhere. He stayed put in Chandigarh and began a new trend in India. Unwittingly, he proved that if one had the capability one could reach the very top from anywhere. Today there are many cricketers who have followed his stirring example, with Dhoni being a glorious example. Although, of course, there are the usual average players who have gone over to other States to take the advantage of powerful lobbies.

In 1979 when Kapil went to Pakistan with Bedi's India team he brought in a breath of fresh air. He batted and bowled differently from others. There was no inhibition apparent in his cricket. No unnecessary bonhomie with opponents on the field. No set theories shackled him. He had no time for preconceived ideas. He was not in the least overawed even in the presence of super-stars. He appeared remarkably relaxed in the hard world of international cricket.

On the fast bowler's burial ground of a wicket at Faisalabad, he made his Test debut. In that series of sorrow when every Indian bowler was torn apart, the young *Jat* captured our imagination. He bowled aggressively and fast. He was not the fastest in the world but was fast enough to make established batsmen duck and weave from his bumpers. His movement, both ways, made them hear the death rattle. When he used the willow, he launched into attack against the likes of Imran Khan and Sarfraz Nawaz.

Surprisingly, Kapil was not accepted wholeheartedly as a captain by certain sections of the media when he became the captain of India. He led the team convincingly enough in West Indies especially at Berbice, where India defeated the world champions in a one-dayer. As a captain he was far more successful than the supposedly more intelligent captains. Yet for his positive nature, which permeated down to his players, there was constant criticism against his captaincy.

In 1983 for the first time India won the world cup. The skipper happened to be Kapil Dev. He led from the front and led without any bias. Till then India was known to be easy fodders in one-dayers. A team where individual success was more important than team result.

Kapil changed the whole concept. He selected players on the basis of individual merit and team's requirement; and not on the basis of 'playing the favourites'. Even top individual players like Gavaskar and Vengsarkar made way for lesser names because of the needs of the team. It required great courage to omit such established and world-class stars. But then Kapil and his manager Maan Singh thought that the balance of the team was more important than anything else. Subsequently the ultimate achievement proved that their strategy was correct.

The way he handled the wobbly medium pacers brought about a distinct new dimension to the game. Established theories of cricket vanished as Kapil proved to that no conventional strategy was permanent. He showed the world what levels of excellence could be achieved by men who possessed the virtues of length, line and movement as opposed to extreme pace. He laid great emphasis on fielding and his mates responded whole-heartedly.

Like most successful captains, he led by example. He carried his team on his shoulders. He inspired others by his own performance. His determination, his discipline motivated others. He wasted no time with bogus theories. Whether with bat or ball he was always in the midst of action.

In the group match against Zimbabwe, India lay in shambles with 5 wickets down for just 17 runs. The sparse crowd at Tonbridge Wells was

Photograph from the match between India and Zimbabwe in the 1983 World Cup that was not televised

thunderstruck. It was at this hour of reckoning that the skipper chose to play the innings of his life. Probably the greatest innings ever played in a one-day international.

He took time to settle down. Then unfolded an innings of guts and determination; class and character. People, who thought that he was a mere slogger with the bat and would not be able to play a responsible innings, were aghast to find that he actually went on to make 175 vital runs against all odds.

For nearly two decades he was among the top all-rounders of the world. His fast-medium bowling made us proud that we too could give back the fire-power in return. His batting was a revelation. He was remarkably orthodox in technique yet extremely attacking.

This unusually aggressive nature of his gave people the impression that his batting was not based on sound principles. Nothing could be further from the truth. He was capable of every stroke in the book and in addition he had a whole repertoire of strokes which were all his own but based on very sound lines. He was a master of the pull stroke, which he executed with the left leg raised in the posture of the dancing Nataraja. Theoretical perfection combined with exuberant execution made him the cynosure of all eyes.

The student seen here as a mentor to his coach: Kapil Dev gives tips to his coach Mr Desh Prem Azad on how to hold the golf club. Mr. Azad was the first cricket Dronacharya of India

He brought all his native ingenuity in his bowling. He worked hard and with sincerity. He listened and applied. Most importantly, he dreamt that he would be a fast bowler.

He never forgot his early mentor Desh Prem Azad (1938 – 2013). Here too he is an exception because in India there has always been a strange reticence to give credit to the men who actually nurture the talented youngsters much before they become established stars.

The unfortunate tendency was to forget the early coaches and to give all the credit to former-players-turned-coaches who had almost nothing to do with the young player's emergence. But Kapil Dev changed all that. In time many young Indians, especially Tendulkar, Dravid and Dhoni felt proud to mention the names of their early mentors. All this happened because one brave man from Haryana had the courage to speak the truth.

There is a genuine fear that the weight of his statistical performance might submerge the magic of his genius. He batted and bowled with abandon and child-like excitement. People flocked to see him because he gave them hope, he gave them dreams and he gave them the thrill of adventure. He made the elderly feel young again. In him, they found solace in a world of cares and caution. He made us walk tall and handsome. He belonged not to any State but to the country. For the first time ever, we had a man who seemed to carry the dreams of a whole nation.

What is at times forgotten is that he was one of the best fielders at a time when Jonty Rhodes was playing. The catch that he took to dismiss Vivian Richards in the world cup final of 1983 was a super-human effort. He actually ran back nearly 30 yards to catch the mistimed pull and thereby set the seal on India's triumph. A natural athlete, he was among the safest of catchers in the slips. He had stamina, speed and an unerring throw from the deep.

A man in a million he has always been. Charming and modest; the simplicity of a real sage. No work was beneath his dignity. No man was his superior. He seemed to have overcome the dreaded disease of egoism.

As a coach however, he was not successful. This was an entirely different role. A passive part for which he did not have the talent. The garb did not fit the persona. To sit outside and devise strategy was not his forte. On the contrary, he was meant to be in the heat of the battle, forcing others to alter their strategies.

Kapil left his imprint on every aspect of cricket. He is India's most complete cricketer in the sense that his all-round ability superseded those of others, the superlative Vinoo Mankad always excepted. Whether batting, bowling or fielding he was always in the forefront. Today when we hear of players, who only bat or bowl, are doing too much work, we merely laugh because we have seen Kapil do everything to do with the game for days and months, season after season.

Not once in his cricket career did he miss a Test match because of injury or for recuperation. Strains and sprains were unknown to him. In his days there were no trainers and physios. Every individual player was expected to know his job and his responsibility. And accordingly, they trained on their own and kept themselves ready for battle. Kapil played round the year for 20 years in peak physical condition.

Kapil's generosity is legendary. People were pleasantly surprised to find that he was a most unlikely super-star. His natural simplicity, gracious manner, easy laughter would floor people. No egoism ever tarnished his pleasant soul. Once in 1980 in a Wills Trophy tie at Chandigarh Sector 16 ground, the international star himself carried buckets of water to the Bengal dressing room because there was no water in the tap. He just would not let me or anybody else hold the bucket.

Another time at Rai in 1976, every evening he would go to visit this writer who had received a hard sweep on his knee while fielding at forward short-leg. The batter happened to be a young all-rounder named Kapil Dev. Yes, that is Kapil Dev, the man with a heart of pure gold.

Has there ever been a greater all-rounder in India than Kapil? Vinoo Mankad, perhaps, but difficult to think of anyone beyond the Haryana man. For close to 20 years he had bowled his heart out on lifeless pitches of the sub-continent. Never had a single top-quality pacer to partner him. Despite such great odds he was an outstanding success. How did he ever achieve what he did? No explanation would suffice. Best to admit, it was nothing short of a miracle. He was an institution. A unique phenomenon. None has been able to emulate him. He is indeed alone at the top of the summit. Rather lonely, yes, but then the genuine geniuses are always lonely figures.

Kapil Dev was and still is a super-hero to millions. But at heart he is a human being. A man of emotion, of sensitivity. He always wore his heart on his sleeve. One could easily make out the man for he never tried to hide his emotion. When his name cropped up in relation to match-fixing, none quite believed it. But the media and the enforcement department had the sadistic pleasure to needle him no end. Ultimately, he was given a clean chit. But the memory rankled. The sensitive man broke down in full view of his millions of admirers. In fact, we admired him more for that. We were happy to see that he made no attempt to hide his emotions. Why should he? He was not a criminal. He had nothing to hide. He had always played straight and simple. Now, why would he do anything different?

He earned our admiration for his frankness and freedom of expression. The great cricketer was a greater human being indeed.

Sachin Tendulkar (1973–)

Was the advent of Sachin Tendulkar an accident of cricket history? He appeared on the Indian cricketing horizon at an hour when the euphoria of the 1983 world cup victory was fast evaporating from the minds of the cricket followers of the country.

Sachin Tendulkar

It was the twilight hour in the annals of Indian cricket. More of darkness than of light. Nausea seemed to have gripped the cricket administration. Far from consolidating on the world cup conquest, the cricketing fraternity passed into the hands of mediocrity, which thrived on petty jealousies and provincial prejudice.

The vitiated atmosphere had to take its toll. Average cricketers, so long in the comforting shade provided by Mohinder Amarnath, Gavaskar,

Vishwanath and Kapil Dev, were unable to raise their level of cricket. Their inflated egos clouded their judgement and ability. Inevitably, India's fortune plummeted and in consequence dissensions, within the team and in the corridors of power, surfaced.

In this depressing scenario, with gloom looming all over, the presence of the curly-haired innocence of a 16-year old raised our curiosity. Within days of his emergence, the diminutive youngster was taking on the world's best by the horns. The Akrams and the Donalds and the Warnes and the Walshs were made to look human. We realized that we were in the presence of a real genius.

The story of Sachin Tendulkar was an epic of enormous proportions and of widest repercussions. When he padded up to bat for India, one-sixth of humanity went out to bat with him. All their frustrations and failures needed a strong shoulder for support. They clung on to him for security. Expectations on Tendulkar mounted. Demands crossed normal limits. The maestro was expected to come to their rescue day in, day out; month after month; year following year. On every occasion he was expected to fulfil their ever-increasing pleadings.

For him there was no rest: no matter the conditions; no matter the situation; no matter the opposition. The bouncy pitches of South Africa or Australia, the grassy wickets of England or New Zealand all came alike to him. The man was expected to relish new challenges, whether he was Muthiah Muralidharan, Shane Warne or Waqar Younus, every day and come out a winner. Invariably enough, he did so more often than not for almost two decades. The man was a marvel, nothing less.

For any great cricketer the pressure of performing consistently causes great stress. Most succumb; very few survive but the scars remain all the same. But in Sachin's case it was totally different. When he went out to bat, he did not go out merely to bat, but to do battle. He went out to defend the honour of his countrymen; for the self-respect of the brown man. On every occasion, he was expected to play the saviour's role and to win the duel. Even Don Bradman, George Headley or Jack Hobbs never had to face this kind of enormous pressure.

Tendulkar began his Test career as a 16-year old against the fearsome pace trio of Imran Khan, Wasim Akram and Waqar Younus in 1989 on Pakistan soil. His demeanour and determination, courage and character were apparent at every stage. His genius flowered with every series since then. The young man almost overnight became a mature adult.

His phenomenal talents made him carry the burden of the team from a very young age. He was never quite nursed. He did not get the time to acquaint. From the very beginning he was expected to play the dual role of saviour and victor. It was indeed a grave and highly unfair responsibility. No hardened hero could ever have achieved what this young man was being asked to do.

But the man in young Tendulkar stepped into the role with the utmost of ease and conviction. For almost half a decade he was indeed the lone ranger with the responsibility of millions to handle. It was only in the mid-1990s that he had the support of batsmen who were able and willing to lessen the load on him. This was indeed ironical. Whereas all great batsmen, with the possible exception of George Headley of West Indies, had excellent support beside them especially at the start of their careers, Tendulkar never really experienced that kind of luxury.

Actually, at the start of his career his support-system was more vocal than valorous. His highly voluble senior partners were known to duck matches to avoid fast bowling; because of grassy tracks; on account of feigned injuries. Once a man fled the scene of battle because he thought he was being insulted! There were others who had no qualms in selling the country! In the midst of such an ambience how did the young warrior fight for the honour of the country? Herein lay his real greatness that in the midst of mediocrity and sabotage, he singularly stood out like a beacon of hope. No wonder, the whole of India took him to heart.

In the early phase of his career some critics thought that he lacked something extra which denied him the big hundreds and the double centuries. But in time Sachin with his phenomenal batting statistics convincingly exhibited that he had all the attributes of the greatest of batters in the world. And, in addition, he had something extra.

Another unfortunate comparison he had to face was with his great predecessor, Sunil Gavaskar. This was most unfortunate. Both reached the pinnacle of their profession in no uncertain manner. Belonging to two different eras, they had to overcome different obstacles. Comparison between players of different eras is obnoxious and serves no fruitful purpose at all. It is best to consider that greats of different eras would have been as great in other eras as well. So too would Sachin and Sunil if they could have exchanged their places. The debate is endless and fruitless as well.

In time the small frame of the man broadened out in the shoulders but the characteristic soft features, fresh face, curly locks still remained to give him a look of child-like innocence. His mannerisms, his speech, his bearing were all ingredients to the saga of purity that he exuded. Even his modelling assignments involving kids reflected the man's holistic nature.

But on the field, he was dynamite personified. Devastating and dominating. Just as nuclear fission is set up by the tiniest of atoms, so it was with the volcanic eruptions that took place with the little maestro at the wicket. The power that he generated was explosive, exciting, entertaining. His awesome power and sense of adventure was more in tune with the rapier thrusts of Everton Weekes and Clyde Walcott; Vivian Richards and Gordon Greenidge.

Sachin was no Indian in his methods. His batsmanship was of the West Indies mould. Never before did an Indian batter treat the ball with such disdain as he did. His strategy was aggression; his weapon, power.

The niceties of grace and conventional techniques were not for the valiant kid of the 1990s Generation.

Tendulkar was born in independent India. An India free from the shackles of colonialism. An India of self-reliance, of candour and confidence. He knew not the insults or the uncertainties, nor the enforced servility of the pre-independence era. He was born free, free to chart his own course.

Thankfully however the child-like face hid a rational mind which understood the sacrifice that the masters – Vijay Merchant, Vijay Hazare and Sunil Gavaskar – had made to lay the foundation on which he was able to build a most impressive super-structure. Aware of his great heritage, he was no less aware of his own great potential.

Unfortunately, in time a quixotic logic did him in as the captain of India. In our country we suffer from an irrational view that the best player in the team is also the best captain. The reason behind this view has never been convincingly explained. But this highly illogical view is extremely popular among the administrators and in the media. This strange reasoning has had many victims in the past and the latest victim was Tendulkar.

Tendulkar was thrust into the national captaincy not by men of vision, but by men who had their own personal fancies and petty focus. He never quite received the tactical wisdom from anyone nor any support from the men in authority, nor did he get the co-operation of all his mates whole-heartedly.

He had two terms as captain of the national team. On either occasion, genuine success eluded him. Thankfully, he himself decided to relinquish the captaincy to concentrate on his batting. It was to his great credit that he could sacrifice the coveted position. This gesture showed the selflessness of the man.

This was indeed a very wise decision. For instinctive players like Tendulkar, the responsibility of captaincy can be a burden at times. These men are brilliant leaders when they are performing well themselves. They inspire, they motivate by leading from the front. By their own deeds and performance. But once they run into rough weather in their personal form, their leadership qualities suffer. Over the years great batsmen have had to face similar dilemma. Men like Wally Hammond, Vivian Richards, Kim Hughes, David Gower and Zaheer Abbas among others.

Later, free from the chains of care and captaincy, the mighty eagle began to soar high once again. The genius of the man could only be marvelled at. Whatever he touched, turned into gold. He showed that he could bowl seam as well as spin with devastating effect. His leg spin and googly were deceptive enough to capture Test wickets. In ODIs too he has bowled vital spells of seam and spin to bring glory to India.

As an opener in the ODIs, he rewrote most of the records for the first wicket. Such was his aggression and class of stroke-play that every opposition around the world acknowledged his superiority. In Test cricket too, the master batsman ever since his debut in 1989 performed with remarkable consistency. His breath-taking stroke-play fetched him thousands of runs all over the world and against every kind of opposition.

The magic of his unique style of batsmanship was awe-inspiring indeed. He was the trend-setter of many an innovation in India. He began the practice of holding the bat low down the handle. He started the technique of hitting under the ball to get over-boundaries over point and gully. He was the first to commence hitting 'the paddle'.

His aggressive intent and all-conquering spirit brought about a new generation of Indians at the crease. A generation which did not hesitate to try out innovative strokes. Taking a leaf out of Gavaskar's book, the young warrior gave us strength. He made us confident of our own abilities. No longer would the Indians be servile to age-old foreign view-points. This happened to be one of Tendulkar's prime contributions to Indian cricket.

The story of Sachin Tendulkar is a saga of contradictions; an epic of surprises. His was an all-conquering approach yet the child-like face was all innocence. He collared the opposition with apology written all over his face. While dominating hardened bowlers, he looked like a lost child. His father was a lecturer, yet he hated academics. School and books repelled him.

The classroom was a prison and the desk, a scaffold. Why should I spend a life in imprisonment, he thought, when the wide world beckoned him with open arms? The world outside the four walls attracted him, the fresh air enchanted him. His mind told him that he should not waste his time living up to the expectations of others, however well-meaning those would be. Ironically, during his playing period of 25 years, he was perpetually living up to the expectations of millions of his countrymen.

Sachin was always very much his own man. He relied on his own judgement and took his own decisions. Hated flatterers, even the flattery of former cricketers. The late Sir Don in his own subtle way acclaimed SRT's genius and that is the ultimate one could hope for in cricket.

Genius is a word that has become a cliché through over use and misuse. But that is the only word that can appropriately describe the multi-faceted talents of this little giant. Volumes have been written on his various skills and doubtless will be in the years to come. But what is of greater relevance is how did the man acquire the mental strength to withstand the pressure of expectations emanating from millions?

Every step of his is still followed by millions. Every sneeze upsets millions. Every twitch of the nose is interpreted and misinterpreted by millions. How does he get the power to overcome the stress? Or, does he feel no stress at all?

Sachin Tendulkar (4th from right, squatting) with former first-class cricketer Kailash Gattani's Star CC team - forerunner to India u-19 teams - at Lord's in 1989

Author's first foray as a selector resulted in identifying the east zone potentials: Sourav Ganguly (extreme left, standing), Sanjoy Das (2nd from right, squatting) and Ranjiv Biswal (2nd from left, squatting)

Vinod Kambli (extreme left, squatting) and Ajay Jadeja (2nd from left, standing) too make a happy scene

My first interaction with the young Sachin was in 1992. He was in England at the time as the first-ever overseas professional for Yorkshire CCC. I happened to be the coach of Kailash Gattani's Star Cricket Club on its tour of UK. Sachin had played for this team in 1988 at the age of 15 and the following year too had made another tour with Gattani. By late 1989, at the age of 16, he made his Test debut for India in Pakistan against the fearsome trio of Imran Khan, Wasim Akram and Waqar Younus.

While our tour was on, Sachin phoned Kailash from Yorkshire to find out how the young boys were doing and if they were good learners.

Honestly, I was quite amazed to observe his sense of belonging and commitment. He himself was just 19 at the time, in a new environment and among hardened professionals. But he was genuinely concerned about how the young Indian cricketers were doing in UK. I asked him, "Are you enjoying your own cricket here?" The young man replied, "Sir, Cricket is not merely enjoyment to me. I worship cricket. It is everything to me. My 24-hour companion."

Over to 2011. By now the man had served his country for more than two decades. IPL 4 was on. I happened to be the match referee in a match involving Sachin Tendulkar's Mumbai Indians and Kumara Sangakara's Deccan Chargers.

Former Rajasthan all-rounder, Kailash Gattani. Gattani established the Star Cricket Club which selected talented young cricketers and took them on annual cricket tours of England from 1987 to 2004

An episode in the match revealed the magnanimity of the man all the more. At the toss, when team-lists were being exchanged between captains, Sangakara bit his lips and indicated that he had forgotten to bring the team list with him! This was a serious issue of code violation. But at that point of time with the whole cricket world looking at us, I did not want to create a scene. I raised my eyebrows at Sachin and he very coolly nodded that he was fine without the list. The whole incident took just a couple of seconds and the toss took place without anyone else realizing what exactly had happened.

This was sportsmanship at its best. For a captain to allow the opposition to delay submitting the team list is unheard of. But Sachin Tendulkar did it with grace and ease. For my part, I asked Kumara Sangakara to get the team list before we left the field. Sachin insisted that he was fine without it but the impeccably mannered Kumara, embarrassed as he was, was full of apologies as he had the team list brought on the field by another player.

Yet another incident is related to IPL 5. This time I found that Sachin was running on the pitch while taking runs. As cricket followers are aware, no batter is allowed to run on the patch between the two sets of stumps, known as the 'protected area'. But Sachin kept doing it more often than not. After the innings was over, as the match referee I asked the umpires if they had noticed Tendulkar's mistake. One of the umpires was Asad Rauf of Pakistan.

Asad laughed at my query, "Rajuji, please don't even think about it. He has been doing this for 20 years. But, you know, no umpire has ever raised a charge against him on this issue because of two reasons. First is that, although he runs straight between the wickets, he never does anything to spoil the condition of the pitch. And secondly, we have such high respect and affection for him that we cannot even visualize raising charges against this gentleman." This is the kind of regard and admiration our Little Master has earned from hardened professionals around the world.

Another issue of IPL 5 stands out in my memory. I had penalized Munaf Patel 50% of his match fees for abusing Aussie umpire Rod Tucker. As captain of Mumbai Indians, Sachin could have come to a 'hearing' to defend his player Munaf Patel. But Sachin did not. The ultimate gentleman Sachin Tendulkar realized that Munaf deserved the heavy fine as punishment. The upright gentleman in him has no time for people, even colleagues, who do wrong and expect sympathy.

In late 1989 the young man made his Test debut. At just 16 years and some days he was among the youngest ever to play Test cricket. The man who put him on the highest platform was none other than Raj Singh Dungarpur, the chairman of selectors at the time. Other selectors raised their voices against him, primarily because of his youth and more so because he was replacing a player of Mohinder Amarnath's calibre. But Rajbhai's personality and persuasive powers finally won them over. And the rest is history, as the cliché goes.

That he survived in that ambience speaks volumes of his character. From 1989 to 2013 (both inclusive) means 25 years of international cricket! This is an index of the man's astounding form and fitness. Never once was he involved in any kind of controversy. Never once was any doubt raised in any quarter of the man's integrity and honesty. His popularity is world over. Even battle-weary opponents have been known to be his ardent admirers.

Comparison with Sir Donald Bradman is inevitable. Sir Don himself acknowledged that his wife had told him that Sachin Tendulkar's batting reminded her of Don's skills with the bat. Like Sir Don in 1948, Tendulkar too announced his own retirement. Like Sir Don, he too retired at 40. But comparisons between geniuses of different eras serve no useful purpose. Geniuses of every generation outclass the rest against all odds. They are not to be compared and contrasted. They are to be treasured and worshipped.

Sachin Tendulkar with Raj Singh Dungarpur

Sachin Tendulkar's social service is hardly ever reported. He works in silence; hates publicity for doing what he wants to do for the downtrodden. His gratitude for his early coach Ramakant Vithal Achrekar is well known. Here is a man who has exchanged views with the best of cricketing brains around the world, but he has not forgotten the man who helped him to lay the firm foundation as a youngster. This is the kind of gratitude you do not get to see in many players, Rahul Dravid and Mahendra Singh Dhoni always excepted.

Sachin's deep respect for seniors is legendary. Time and again he has mentioned that Sunil Gavaskar's mentorship had helped him. He has the highest regard for former players and makes it a point to keep himself informed about them. In a country where Test cricketers are rated to be the only experts on the game, Sachin holds the opposite view.

He himself was thrust on top not by any former international player, but by a first-class cricketer by the name of Raj Singh Dungarpur. Sachin has not forgotten the contribution of Achrekar and Raj Singh, both non-international cricketers. Even now, striding at the pinnacle of cricket kingdom, he still has a wave, a smile and often a word for the back-stage people who are associated with the game, whether they be umpires, referees, support staff, scorers, administers or players.

Ramakant Achrekar coaching young Sachin

Cradled in the best tradition of Mumbai cricket, Sachin grew up in the strong Marathi stronghold of Shivaji Park in Dadar, which has given birth to numerous cricketers of outstanding calibre. The Mumbai school of cricket is a hard taskmaster but a very fair one: the deserving gets enough opportunities of match-play, immediate recognition of talent and genuine encouragement from the right quarters. No favours are granted, and none is expected.

Indian cricket lovers owe a debt of gratitude to Sachin's elder brother, Ajit. Ajit was the person who first understood that Sachin preferred the outdoors to the confines of a classroom.

One incident revealed the character of the man. It was an IPL match in 2011 at Hyderabad. I was having a glass of *lassie* around 11am in the hotel room, when a very excited room-service staff came in to say, "Mr. Tendulkar is in his room down the corridor. He is not having any food today because Sai Baba is no more." Switched on the television to find that Satya Sai's soul had left the world early morning.

At the ground Sachin looked very forlorn. Played the match and then went by road all the way from Hyderabad to Puttaparthi in Andhra Pradesh, arriving early next morning. The commitment to his team; the commitment to the paying spectators and the devotion to Satya Sai were all encapsulated in splendid isolation without any fuss. Amazing person, indeed.

Sachin with Ajit

Now that the little-master-turned-great-batsman has retired from active cricket, I salute him for the wonderful time he gave us. He helped Indian cricket to earn universal respect and admiration.

Statesmen

Polly Umrigar (1926–2006)

Polly Umrigar was the chief architect who laid the stolid foundation of modern Indian cricket. He had time for every cricketer from the junior-most to the former players. Nothing in Indian cricket was beyond his knowledge and extreme involvement.

Polly Umrigar

Former Test cricketers have been remarkably unsuccessful as cricket administrators. Only a handful has left behind any worthwhile contribution. Most former cricketers-turned administrators succumbed to the machination of the officials they replaced. Transparency, visionary approach, cricketers' welfare, youth programmes were anathema to them. They merely carried out the age-old policies of their short-sighted predecessors and personal aggrandizement.

There were some glorious exceptions, though. But none more convincing than the visionary Polly Umrigar. As the BCCI secretary, from his small office at an obscure corner of CCI's Brabourne Stadium, he thought big. As a student of cricket, he was the ultimate servant of the game. To use a cliché, he slept, ate and drank cricket.

No, he did not stop at that. It was not oxygen but cricket that he drew in with every breath. What came out from him was all-embracing wisdom: youth coaching camps around the country, national cricket academies,

improvements in travel and accommodation for youth teams, awards for different age-groups, efforts to promote cricket in north-east India, welfare schemes for former cricketers, etcetera.

Today when former Test and first-class cricketers are enjoying the benefits of the BCCI pension scheme, little do they realize that the man who made it possible was Polly Umrigar with active assistance from Raj Singh Dungarpur, a former first-class cricketer himself. It is my great fortune that both Polly Kaka and Raj Bhai had imposed a lot of faith in me as we meddled around with the modalities of the intended pension scheme in 1990s.

In the mid-1990s when Umrigar was firmly in the BCCI secretary's saddle, he conceived the idea of providing pension to former cricketers. He had all the papers and files ready with the budgets, eligibility criteria, mode of payment and other formalities for the BCCI top administrators to see and sign. When I raised an issue concerning cricketers' widows, Raj Bhai joked, "Raju does not have me in mind!"

The BCCI administrators took eight long years to come to terms to assist people who had helped the country's cricket to prosper. This too came about with the arrival of Sharad Pawar at the helm. Thankfully BCCI's full-time administrator Professor Ratnakar Shetty was near at hand to show Union Minister Sharad Pawar, the new BCCI president, the documents that Polly Umrigar had so lovingly prepared and preserved.

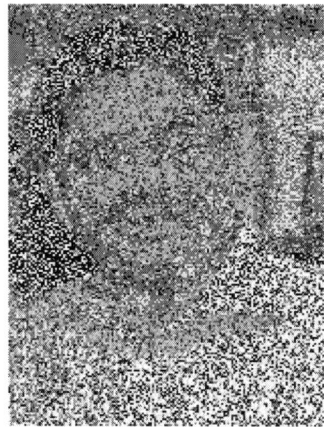

Wonder-Man of Indian Cricket: Professor Ratnakar Shetty, prime innovator of BCCI's visionary schemes

Unfortunately, Polly Umrigar's magnanimous approach to assist former cricketers was never highlighted in India. Even BCCI presidents, who had kept the files under wraps since the mid-1990s, took credit and shelved the name of the genuine creator from the media and the people. Today every former cricketer should take time to say a short prayer for the soul who made so many families happy. I knew I did not make a mistake in identifying my all-time hero.

No schoolboy fiction was ever conceived without the wide shoulders, the clear-cut features and the booming voice which went on to make the hero's personality. We had come to believe that such qualities were found only in story books. But in Polly Umrigar's story, it was no fiction. It was as authentic as the city of Mumbai which had nurtured and nourished him.

Christened Pahlan Rattanji Umrigar, the man was a larger-than-life persona. The massive frame sheltered a heart still bigger. Never, not even once did those shoulders stoop. Rather, those were strong enough to perpetually carry his peers. His magnanimous presence captivated all and sundry.

As a child I had often seen him playing the dour role of saving India from embarrassment. But the first distinct impression that remains was that of a leader harnessing his men to victory. The year was 1961–62; the venue, Eden Gardens and the opposition Ted Dexter's England (then MCC). Polly Umrigar was not the appointed captain. But in skipper Nari Contractor's absence, he introduced Ramakant Desai from the High Court end and brought about the downfall of the prolific Ken Barrington. Desai bounced, Barrington hooked and Durani, at square leg, made the difficult catch look easy.

That masterpiece of tactics had the floodgates open and England collapsed giving India her first-ever Test match victory at Eden Gardens. As the dignified figure of Polly Umrigar receded into the pavilion, he walked into the pantheon of cricket history. Never before or after has a deputy captain made such an inspiring move to liven up an almost dead Test match.

Later I met him in 1976 when he was a national selector and I was a Bengal player. During the course of the Eden Gardens Test match, he and colleagues wanted to have a look at the Test prospects from East Zone. Very hastily a net session was organized. All the national selectors, except the eastern region representative, turned up as did the potential players. But none bothered to prepare the pitch for the net session to take place! National selector from Central Zone Kisan Rungta was furious at the callousness of the local cricket administration. Polly Umrigar was shocked and sympathized, "Hope you boys are more fortunate next time." Later as the BCCI secretary, he took every possible step for the promotion of youth cricket so that no cricket talent would be lost through carelessness.

After my cricketing days were over, I kept in touch with Polly Kaka. I would write to him very often with proposals and suggestions. Not once did he express any botheration. On the contrary he would write back words of encouragement and discuss cricket issues.

In the late 1990s when he was the BCCI secretary, Polly Kaka actually came to watch an under-16 inter-zone one-day tournament (then the Vijay Hazare Trophy). When my trainees went on to win the trophy, he was gracious enough to be present with words of encouragement. Can you imagine an influential, senior BCCI official coming to the ground to encourage under-16 talents? None has done it yet.

Sir Garfield Sobers was undoubtedly the greatest of all-rounders. He was a rare 3-in-1 all-rounder; a person capable of bowling pace and spin as well as batting. But was he the first of the 3-in-1s? Surely not. That credit, arguably, may be conferred on Polly Umrigar, the most underrated of our sporting heroes. About his batting and of-spinning abilities legends abound, but his medium paced out-swingers and off-cutters did not receive the recognition those deserved.

At a time when India did not possess top-class pace bowlers, we had to rely on the incisive medium pacers of this burly all-rounder from

Mumbai. Hardly ever he disappointed. On the matting wicket of Bahawalpur in 1954–55 against Pakistan he enjoyed his best spell with the new ball: 58–25–74–6.

No Indian cricket addict has quite been able to shed the pangs of recrimination at the way Umrigar was treated by the national selectors and the media. He was a natural leader of men. A man of dominating presence and astute thinking. At the same time, understanding and considerate. He was not the kind to create a halo of impregnability around himself to unnerve the uninitiated. Nor would he have a permanent nod for the powers-that-be. He belonged to neither group and invariably suffered the consequences. For his uncompromising posture, he was our hero.

Against Harry Cave's New Zealand in 1955–56, Umrigar's India won the series 2 nil. Next winter he went about consolidating the team as the nucleus was rapidly ageing. But constant changing and chopping did not help to cement the team's morale against Ian Johnson's Australia as the series was lost. But the imposing personality never stooped not even against the marauding West Indies, who had the blistering pace of Wesley Hall and Roy Gilchrist and the genius of Rohan Kanhai and Garfield Sobers. The team brought off an honourable draw in the first Test, but the strength of the opposition created an inferiority complex among the players. Umrigar realized the problem soon enough and requested the selectors for a few changes. He wanted courageous men who would fight till the end even for a lost cause. But the selectors refused to yield and Polly Umrigar, the man of high principles, relinquished the captaincy. No Indian captain before or since has shown such sterling qualities of character.

However, to his eternal credit he never bore grudges, nor did he brood himself to frustration. He served under Mansur Ali Khan Pataudi, 15 years his junior, and wholeheartedly supported the young captain in West Indies in 1962. In Pataudi's *Tiger's Tale*, the unhesitating help of Polly Umrigar has been mentioned. Umrigar played under various captains of very average leadership ability but not once did he show any rancour, nor did he ever try to scheme to get his captaincy crown back.

A grave injustice was done to him by a flippant remark which went on to become an international headline. He had a dismal series in England in 1952. To compound matters it was said that he had backed away from the express deliveries of Freddie Trueman. If that was true, then so were many eminent names in international cricket. Did not the Australians fall in a heap against Peter Pollock in South Africa in 1970? Did not the Englishmen draw away from Lillee and Thompson in Australia? There are numerous similar examples. Why was Umrigar singled out? But the fact remains that he went back to England in 1959 and collared Trueman and Harold Rhodes and smashed an innings of 118 at Old Trafford. He took on the mighty Wes Hall in his own backyard with an unbeaten innings of 172. Where were those who had derided the callow youth on his first tour in 1952? He was never media savvy and never cared about what the uninitiated thought of him.

Against Fazal Mahmood's men he had his most successful series ever. He reeled off 3 centuries in 5 Tests. No matter the opposition, no matter the conditions, Umrigar was a man for all seasons. When he retired in 1962 he had a fantastic average of 42.22 with 3631 runs including 12 centuries. As a bowler he never got his due. Overshadowed by the presence of Vinoo Mankad, Ghulam Ahmed and Subhash Gupte, he was always considered to be a second fiddle. Yet when the Aussies capsized against Jasu Patel at Kanpur in 1959, it was Polly Umrigar's 4 vital wickets including those Neil Harvey and Norman O'Neil that hastened the disaster. As a fieldsman he was of the top bracket, whether close to or far from the wicket. A safe pair of hands, a strong throw and impeccable anticipation were his hallmarks.

After retirement from active cricket, he was even more active in the service of the game. As coach, manager, administrator he left behind his mark in every sphere and was highly respected by all those who came in contact with him. Deep knowledge and a broad mind gave him a wider vision than usual. Remarkably open to views he would take suggestions even from laymen. Very diligently he studied and then made his recommendations to BCCI. It was primarily because of his initiative that former players, both Test and first-class, are receiving pension from BCCI in recognition of their services to Indian cricket.

The modesty of the man was profound. Once I met him at Sunil Banerjee's place in Calcutta. Polly Kaka had read a piece of mine on him in Pataudi-edited *Sportsworld* and thanked me profusely, "Raju, that article of yours pleasantly surprised my family. They thought no one remembered me anymore. Next time you come to Mumbai you must have a cup of tea with us." With his demise, I have lost the man whom I respected the most in Indian cricket.

Polly Umrigar's retirement from cricket as an active player had a unique ring about it. After scores of 56,172 not out, 32 and 60 against Hall, Sobers and Gibbs he decided that he had had enough. People were aghast. They kept asking, "Why?" Polly Umrigar's classic reply was, "Better now when they are asking 'why' than later when they would be asking 'why not'. Indeed, indeed. What a lesson from a champion sportsman. His action taught us what character was; what wisdom meant.

Rahul Dravid (1973–)

The first time I met Rahul Dravid was at Mumbai in 2005–06. The occasion was the inaugural edition of BCCI's T20 tournament. BCCI's inter-stateT20 tournament is named after the memory of one of India's master batsmen, Syed Mushtaq Ali. The match was at Wankhede Stadium and one of the teams happened to be Karnataka.

The day before the match at the pre-match meeting, where the two contesting teams meet the umpires and the match referee, Karnataka was represented by their new captain Yere Gowda, as the original captain Dravid was not certain to

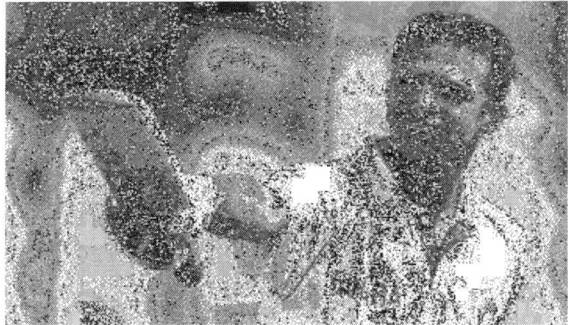

Rahul Dravid

play. At the time he was leading India and the national team had just returned from a foreign tour and so the Karnataka manager Sudhakar Rao informed us that their original choice as captain, Rahul Dravid, may not be able to arrive on time for the match.

Next morning, before the toss while the umpires and I, as the match referee, were inspecting the pitch, we saw that Rahul Dravid was walking towards the pitch. As he came near, he exchanged pleasantries and then was about to step on the pitch itself. I quickly blurted out, "Are you leading the team in this match?" He shook his head and said, "No." I smiled and added, "Probably you have forgotten that as a playing member you are not supposed to walk on the pitch. Only the captain has the prerogative."

Instantly he stopped and said, "I am sorry. Thanks for reminding me." I replied, "Cannot blame you, Rahul. As the India captain you have got used to walking on the pitch before the match. Anyway, no harm done. Thanks."

Suddenly the huge frame of Venkatesh Prasad appeared. He thought I was having a confrontation with Rahul Dravid. He shrugged his shoulders and raised his voice at me, "Do you realize that you are arguing with the India captain." Without a moment's hesitation, the India captain Rahul Dravid cut him short, "Ref is correct. As an ordinary player I am not allowed on the pitch."

This is the real Rahul Dravid. A man of courage; a man of character. Courageous enough to accept that he himself was about to make a mistake. He had no qualms in saying so in front of the curator, the umpires and others who were near us at the time. Revealed exemplary character to silence his colleague for being wrong. I feel proud to see that we still have such men in India.

Later that evening, after our match was over I went across to the Brabourne Stadium, the home of Cricket Club of India (CCI), to watch another T20 match in progress. As I entered, Dilip Vengsarkar called me over to the seat beside him. On the other side of Vengsarkar was Rahul Dravid.

Vengsarkar introduced me to him saying, "Meet my friend Raju." Straight-faced Dravid replied, "Met him this morning. A very lenient match referee." When Dilip furrowed his eyebrows to know what had transpired earlier, Rahul smiled and mentioned the incident. Dilip added sauce, "Even when he was playing he behaved like a match ref."

As the conversation flowed, Rahul mentioned that he had liked reading my book, "The part about cricket being played during Mahabharata days was an eye-opener." I was astounded that he had found the time to read my writing. As if this was not enough, he added, "Rajan Bala told me to read your articles. I usually do." He was so very matter of fact. No ego. No pretence. I came to learn that he was an avid collector of cricket books.

Later that season, again our paths crossed. This time again at Wankhede. The occasion was a Ranji Trophy tie between Mumbai and Karnataka. Before leaving Calcutta, I had taken a first edition Cardus duplicate that I had in my collection for Rahul. My wife Seema was mad at me, "Do you realize that you would be giving the India captain a moth-eaten, old book? What will he think of you?" I had told her before departure, "If any player would realize its worth, that would be Dravid."

How correct I was. The moment he had the tattered copy in his hands, he uttered, "Are you sure you want to part with this original edition Cardus? This is a collector's item. This will be a treasure in my collection." The cerebral man did not bother about the non-glossy exterior. Here was a man who could buy new books from all over the world. But he understood the value of antiquity.

Another incident revealed the man all the more. At Mysore city Karnataka were hosting Punjab to a Ranji Trophy tie. Manish Pandey, a young talented batter, was playing an excellent innings and remained unbeaten on 80 at the end of the penultimate day, with his team needing around 50 plus to win the tie. While they were doing their cooling-down drills, I called Pandey and asked him the reason for wearing light grey coloured shoes while batting. Skipper Rahul was more embarrassed than the culprit, Pandey. Rahul, however, asked me if it was possible to allow him to continue with those shoes as he had no other pair.

I told Dravid that if he felt it was perfect, I would allow Pandey to continue with those shoes. Rahul replied, "No, no I do not think these shoes are ok. He should be wearing white shoes. Will you please accept if he puts white plaster on the shoes while batting?" I understood the problem, "Fair enough, skip. Out of sheer respect for you, I will allow it."

Next day Pandey got his hundred and Karnataka won the match. After the conclusion, skipper Rahul came to the referee's room and thanked me, "You have opened my eyes. I found most of my lads do not possess proper white cricket shoes. I assure you from next match Karnataka players will wear absolutely proper white shoes." I was stunned to say the least. Here was a captain who had the courtesy to acknowledge even a minor problem and willing to admit it in public. Not many captains would uphold the traditional values of cricket in this manner.

Another incident revealed another dimension of his persona. At Jaipur, Rajasthan Royals was involved in a match with Delhi Daredevils. It was an IPL match in 2012. As match referee, I walked in for the toss. The commentator was Sanjay Manjrekar. He asked me, "Sir, I just want to get the pronunciation of your name correctly. Is it MUKHERJI?" He proceeded to repeat my surname so that he got the pronunciation right. Instantly Dravid, the RR skipper, smiled, "No, his real name is not MUKHERJI. It is MUKHOPADHYAY. " I was taken aback for a moment, then replied, "Rahul is absolutely right. Since I am in tie and jacket I call myself Mukherji. In dhoti-kurta, I call myself Mukhopadhyay." With a smile, Rahul wagged his finger at Sanjay meaning I told you so.

The man is really amazing. How did he come to know that the Mukherjis are actually Mukhopadhyays!! For a man from Karnataka to know the origin of Bengali surnames is quite astounding. His awareness of the world around goes far beyond the comprehension of most sportsmen. Bright, well-read and articulate, the man is actually one in a million.

Rahul Dravid is a man of gratitude. He is known to have told the world time and again that Keki Tarapore was his coach, even though he has come under the guidance of far more famous cricket personalities. I asked Shahir Tarapore, the

Rahul Dravid as a schoolboy cricketer.
Standing fourth from left

former first-class cricketer and eminent international umpire about Dravid's relationship with his father.

My friend Shahvir said, "My father was his coach at school. Rahul never let anybody forget that. He kept in constant touch with dad even when he was busy with his very tight international schedule. Dad used to feel a little embarrassed when Rahul often praised him publicly. But Rahul always maintained that the early coaches were the real coaches for they help to lay the foundation. To have a proper structure, you need a solid foundation." How very true. But how many famous players (Sachin Tendulkar and MS Dhoni always excepted) would acknowledge the fact that they should be indebted to their early coaches? Only a man of rare character would have the broad-mindedness to accept the truth.

Dravid's greatness as a batsman needs no elaboration. Completely selfless, he even volunteered to keep wickets for India. People who have not played the game would not realize how very difficult it is for a non-regular wicket-keeper to do this role and then to succeed at his primary job of batting as well. Rahul achieved the extremely difficult task most commendably and without a word of annoyance.

As a leader of men, he proved himself time and again for India. He won Test series in West Indies and in England. Not many Indian captains have achieved this rare feat of winning against major teams overseas.

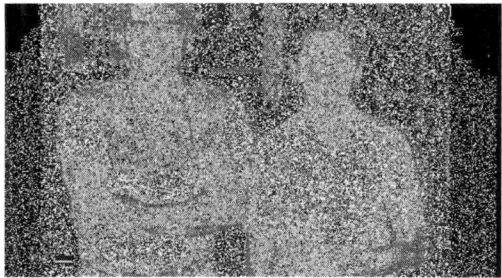

Rahul Dravid as a schoolboy cricketer
with Sunil Gavaskar

Initially with Karnataka and later with Rajasthan Royals, captain Dravid kept his profile low but was highly proactive. He was their captain, their mentor, their coach. He accepted every role with grace and graciousness. Players within his orbit progressed not only as cricketers but also as human beings. All those who have played under him whether for Karnataka or Rajasthan Royals have no qualms in acknowledging that they literally worship him.

Rahul Dravid remained the modest self that he had always been. Never a word out of place. Never an act to raise any eyebrow. Never cared for publicity. Never flirted with any controversy. Never tried to draw any attention to himself. Always remained the selfless, low-profile, intelligent and articulate gentleman. In a cricket world that had lost its innocence, Dravid's presence was the only consolation. He upheld the spirit of cricket and its traditional values on and off the field. He was probably the last of a rare breed. A great cricketer; a greater human being.

Rahul Dravid belongs to the Age of Renaissance. He does not believe in the violent radicalism of change, but in the matured reasoning of fusion. His approach is the approach of an intelligent, enquiring mind. A mind that observes, listens, studies, absorbs. A mind that is willing to probe and to question and to discuss. A mind that acknowledges the contribution of the past; a mind that seeks the path of future progress.

As a pragmatic individual, like the heroes of the Renaissance, his whole cricket was based on the fundamental values and classical ideas of the game. He used the full face of the bat to the ball because that was the original idea of the game. It has not changed because the width of the bat remains the same. He did not believe in snicking a ball and claiming to have guided the ball on purpose. I have seen him lower his head in disappointment and in anguish when an edged, unintended shot fetched him some runs.

When he played forward, he almost embraced the ball close to his body. Knees and waist sufficiently bent, not in supplication but with all due concentration for the job. Like the classical exponents he wanted his mind and his eyes to monitor the movement of his body to the ball. This was concentration and commitment of the highest order. No one in the whole wide world could cut and pull in the classical manner that he was capable of. His batting was based on firm, conventional principles.

Early in his career his solid foundation allowed him to play cricket in an orthodox manner which attracted the connoisseur. So successful was he that he became a prisoner of his own image: the man with a solid defensive technique. Unfortunately, some former cricketers-turned-experts praised his defensive technique to such an extent that his defensive technique became a chain around his neck. He developed a defensive approach — as different from defensive technique — and consequently his progress as a batsman was halted. He found it difficult to score fast, even to rotate the strike with quick singles. So engrossed was he with his copy-book approach — whatever that meant — that he lost his lovely strokes and just could not dominate the bowling. In the one-dayers, his batting actually appeared to be a liability at times.

The team management, around this time requested him to keep wickets so that he would remain in the XI and the balance of the team would be maintained. Initially he was a little uncertain but then his intelligence told him to take up the challenge to accept the role of the wicket-keeper in the one-day team. This is indeed a tribute to his character and approach that he was willing to shoulder the responsibility for the sake of the country.

Typical of the short-sighted nature of our experts, Dravid was advised by quite a few people not to keep wickets as that, they claimed, would affect his batting! Why would the art of wicket-keeping affect someone's batting has never been convincingly explained!! There have been so, so many world-class cricketers — Clyde Walcott, Denis Lindsay, Adam Gilchrist and specially Kumar Sangakara to name a few – who have done both the jobs so well that such an argument reveals gross ignorance. Thankfully, Dravid was quick to grasp that he was being misled or that he was being underestimated.

The result of Dravid's acceptance of the dual role became apparent when he revealed remarkable progress not only in his wicket-keeping skills but also in his positive approach to batting. The improvement came about because of the man's attitude, application and intelligence. This aggressive intent in his one-day batting gave him a fresh lease of life even in Tests. The real Rahul Dravid finally stood up tall and handsome in the face of adversity.

Dravid was a champion cricketer of the old school: impeccable technique, both in defence and in offence. A man who carried the national flag on his shoulders. An Indian national of pride and self-respect. Rare qualities to have in those days of match-fixing and bribery.

In the late 1990s Indian cricket was in doldrums. The match-fixing charge had exposed some. The internal intrigues were still visible. Thankfully the BCCI decided on a change of image. They would have players and coaches whose integrity was beyond question. Refreshing changes came up. Dravid's suggestion to have foreign coaches was accepted. His recommendation of his former Kent coach, John Wright, was a master-stroke. It annoyed some former cricketers who were viewing the monetary benefits, but it did help to catapult Indian cricket into the big league.

Now, the Indian team began to believe that it could win. Earlier India would play for individual records but now it is the team's achievement that takes precedence over personal glory. It all began with a bold decision by Dravid, stand-in skipper for Ganguly in the Multan Test against Pakistan in 2004, to declare the Indian innings closed when Sachin Tendulkar was unbeaten on 194.

This singular act of courage and pragmatism at Multan by the stand-in skipper Rahul Dravid changed the course of cricket leadership in India. Now personal interest became totally secondary to the team's cause. Thankfully in time Dhoni and Kohli maintained the positive outlook.

Dravid's early tryst with the India captaincy was not very convincing. He seemed apprehensive, uncertain, a trifle hesitant and also to lack the spirit of leadership. But at

Rahul Dravid as the Indian captain against England

Multan he was a rejuvenated captain. Took a very bold decision and stood by it. The decision was taken for the benefit of the team and not for any individual's personal interest. This is the winning-formula that has recently developed in the India team for which every member can rightfully take the credit. This kind of approach was not always in existence in the past and consequently team interest suffered on many occasions.

Dravid has been a marvellous statesman for cricket as well as for India. Well-read, sensitive, he has approached his job of playing for India from various angles. Primarily, as a cricketer. But, no less important, as a national representative. Whether meeting young fans or heads-of-state he has kept his perspectives clear. Many prejudicial critics tried to wean him away from his unbiased and liberal approach. It is to Dravid's great credit that he did not fall into the trap of his flatterers. He had the sense to visualize that every individual has his own strength and weakness.

Instead of forming groups and resorting to conspiracies, skipper Dravid remained his own man. He kept his head, followed his intuition and conveyed to all around him that he would back his own intelligence and judgement rather than rely on those who attempted to sabotage the nation's interest through prejudice and cunning.

The man's selfless service to Indian cricket would be remembered by those who have seen him. For future generations his contribution would be enshrined in diamond and platinum. Rahul Dravid's serious mien is reflected in the frown that he wears. It is not the frown of a disturbed man, but the frown of a man of commitment. A soul, who is willing to make personal sacrifices for the national cause. What a refreshing change of attitude he introduced from those petty men who dropped themselves under various pretext and strange ailments; and from men who created hassles even about batting orders and bowling spells. His has been an approach that lends credence to conventional and orthodox patterns. An approach that reassures the older generation to keep faith in the younger set.

The man's consistency with the bat was a tribute to his technique and temperament. Today his contribution as a coach of the junior India teams has yet again revealed his consistency-factor, his unbiased-approach, his positive-nature, his sincere commitment and his enjoyment-issue without sacrificing the earnestness.

He is a model to emulate; a model to rejoice about. Our national pride. A man who enriched the game of cricket as Charles Burgess Fry had done in the early 20th century.

MS Dhoni (1981–)

In 2004 the BCCI began a system by which young talented cricketers around the country would be identified and short-listed for further training. The idea germinated from the fertile brain of Makarand Waingankar, the highly conscientious freelance journalist from Mumbai. Makarand, very rightly, thought that young players from the distant corners of the country were being neglected by the BCCI and consequently by the junior and senior national selectors.

MS Dhoni

Former senior first-class cricketers were appointed by the BCCI to watch every representative BCCI match, junior and senior, and to identify and inform the Board of potential talents for the junior and senior national teams. PC Poddar and I travelled to Jamshedpur to watch the players in action in the one-day senior inter-state championship in January 2004.

At the end of the first day's match, Poddar and I went out to have our evening meal. While discussing cricket, Poddar blurted out, "Today I saw a man hitting the ball with awesome power. Never before have I seen anybody with such immense power in his strokes." Coming from a man of Poddar's deep knowledge and wide experience, I was extremely keen to have

Makarand Waingankar

a good look. Poddar added, "Tomorrow you would be watching the Bihar match. Have a good look at the opener with long hair."

Next morning, as I alighted from the taxi near the Keenan Stadium pavilion gate, I found a motor-cycle screech to a halt a few metres away. A well-built lad in his mid-20s wearing a tight tee-shirt and denims parked his vehicle. Instantly two pariah dogs came towards him and he brought out some biscuits from his pocket to feed them. The speeding bike, the long flowing hair style, the bulging biceps all mitigated against the sensitive care that he took to show his affection for the road-side canines.

I asked Kanu Chakravarty, the Bihar coach, if he was the opener who hit the ball very hard. Kanuda replied, "In my Bihar team everybody hits the ball hard. But this boy from Ranchi is an exceptionally hard hitter. He is actually a wicket-keeper/batsman, playing first-class cricket for about 4 years. No one has ever taken any notice of him yet. Why are you so keen to know about him?" By the end of the day, when he had scored just about 40 odd, I realized that I had seen an uncut diamond.

That evening both Poddar and I exchanged notes. We decided to send our report to the chief Talent Resource Development Officer (TRDO), Dilip Vengsarkar, specially mentioning the batting ability and the exceptional power of the young man's strokes. As it transpired, the responsible people at the BCCI took serious note of the report and the career graph of a young talent from a neglected corner of India took an upward curve.

By the end of the very year – 2004 – MS Dhoni was playing for India and had done enough to cement his place. Other wicket-keepers, who hailed from favoured provinces and were being played in the national team by turns and on whims, were now vying for the reserve stumper's post. A new star had risen on the horizon.

Young players around the country began to realize that for the advancement of their own careers, the TRDO system was a significant step forward. Almost overnight, as it were, the sincere efforts of the

TRDOs began to show results. Men of the calibre of Suresh Raina, Irfan Pathan, among others, came into prominence. The TRDO system in the hands of sincere men brought instant results to Indian cricket. Other sports would do well to follow the BCCI in this respect. A nursery of unknown talent would flower within days.

Dhoni's career graph is a unique case in Indian cricket. Hailing from a family of very modest financial background, he had little option but to accept whatever job came his way. The Indian Railways gave him a job based at Kharagpur at the border of Bengal and Orissa but, true to tradition, decided that a man from the eastern region would not be good enough for the all-India Railways cricket team!

The Railways recruited him for his cricket ability, yet it appeared they had no faith in their own choice! The Railway employee MS Dhoni never got a look-in from the very people who were given the responsibility to handle the Railway cricket team!

Since Dhoni was based at Kharagpur, which happens to be in West Bengal, he was very much qualified to represent Bengal in national championships. Where were the Bengal selectors – all former test and first-class cricketers – at the time? Their job was to select the best of talent residing in Bengal. Were they doing their job? Or, were they only concerned about extracting favours from influential quarters?

As disappointing were the selectors of East Zone. Although Dhoni had already played for no less than 4 years for Bihar in first-class cricket, not one selector – zonal or national – ever thought that this man had some exceptional ability in him!

Such were the former cricketers who were entrusted with the job to identify talent.

Dhoni's school coach,
Keshav Banerjee

Lack of integrity and the desire to be pressurized by influential lobbies seemed to be the ideal qualities to be a selector in India, both at the zonal and national levels. Ironical to relate, Dhoni was in the same zone as the India captain, Sourav Ganguly, and had played against him at the time.

The tough, talented youth had little exposure to the 'big names' of Indian cricket when he was at Ranchi and Jamshedpur. He picked up the finer points from various sources as he went along without ever forgetting his first school coach, "Banerjee Sir" as Dhoni still most respectfully addresses him. He kept his ears and eyes open in the India dressing room to observe what Tendulkar and Dravid were doing to prepare themselves for the battles ahead. Off the field, his cool and composed personality was the just right ingredient required for a person craving to learn the ways of the world.

During an IPL match, as match referee I requested the Chennai Super King skipper Dhoni to call very loudly at the toss because the extremely high decibel music from the stands could plug one's ears. Dhoni, true to his impeccable manners, said, "Do not worry, sir. I will call 'tails'." He was, it goes without saying, true to his promise.

The author as a match referee in IPL with MS Dhoni and Mahela Jayawardene

Reams have been devoted to his exceptional abilities. I shall not repeat those to irritate my readers. But I would like to relate that never before have we had a leader in India as exemplary as the man from Ranchi. He led India to the inaugural T20 world cup trophy with all the top names of Indian cricket dropping out of the team for one reason or other! A young set of keen lads helped the relaxed captain to bring off one victory after another.

Before leading India, did MS Dhoni ever lead a cricket team? Perhaps his school team. But, even then, I doubt it. Because he was first and foremost a football goalkeeper. It was only when his school coach, Keshav Ranjan Banerjee, asked him to become the school keeper, did he pick up the wicket-keeping gloves. Surely you do not give the captaincy to a replacement player? Dhoni had no experience of captaincy; no grooming at all. It seemed he did not need any. Players instinctively followed him for his sterling qualities of character. A distinct sign of a born, natural leader of men.

The magnificent man went on lead India to the world ODI title which only skipper Kapil Dev was able to achieve in 1983. As if these crowns were not enough, Dhoni led India to become the numero uno in the Test rankings. No other Indian captain has been able to match these statistical highlights. In fact, has any other captain from any country been able to hold all the three trophies at the same time?

Despite such magnificent achievements, the cool and composed man still remains as modest and accessible as he was nearly two decades back when he was making his debut in first-class cricket for Bihar. Far from stooping to gamesmanship, he was the epitome of the 'spirit of cricket' concept. His classic calling back of Ian Bell in England will forever remain a great lesson in sportsmanship. He even allowed a re-toss after having won the first toss in a world cup final. A sage, no less.

Never took advantage of his position. He could have promoted players of his choice or his State but never did. He respected the selectors and allowed them to do their job. Never got involved with any publicity stunts. Never bothered to get into conflicts and controversies. Detested sledging and avoided verbal duels. Never resorted to any kind of one-upmanship. He was and still remains a champion in the truest sense of the word.

His persona was and still is such that people consider him to be the leader, whether he is leading the team or not. He gave up his Test position so that Wriddhiman Saha could come in. He did it in style and in isolation. Did not create any hullaballoo about it. How many men, dear reader, you know who has given up the India captaincy voluntarily without any pressure? None till Dhoni showed us the way. A neglected man from an obscure corner showed the so-called 'metropolitan' Indians what actual magnanimity was all about. It was only because of his generosity that the crown prince Virat Kohli could be gradually groomed for the leadership seat.

It is to the great credit of Virat Kohli that he has shown the highest possible respect to his benefactor. In the dressing room, Dhoni in his quiet and low-profile manner is still a great influence on other cricketers. Just as chief coach Ravi Shastri and the captain Kohli readily admit Dhoni's reassuring presence, every young player makes a beeline for his guidance.

After being out of the captaincy throne, no other India captain has earned the respect and affection of his peers as Dhoni has. This shows the man's actual worth. Even when not in the any seat of power his considerable aura pervades every nook and corner of Indian cricket. People from all walks of life revere the man for what he is. The media flocks to him. The sponsors crowd around him. Powerful politicians want to shake hands with him. Film stars have been known to be photographed with him. He does not, and never did, go out to seek publicity or power; fame or fortune. Everything comes to him because he deserves it. When not actively involved with the national team, Dhoni still finds the time to be with his Jharkhand players at the ground. He does not need any official appellation, but he becomes everyone's mentor. His accessibility, his easy manner, his ready smile are not artificial at all. Spontaneous, modest, sincere, honest that is what he was and, thankfully, still remains so.

No fiction writer would ever have conceived the rise and rise of Dhoni to fame and fortune. He was nowhere on the radar in early 2004 before two talent spotters of BCCI strongly recommended his name to their chief. Thankfully the India 'A' selectors had a close look and realized his potential. Without wasting time, they put the 23-year old, as the reserve wicket-keeper, on the plane to Kenya and Zimbabwe with the India 'A' team in mid-2004. With the main wicket-keeper Dinesh Kartik 'called' to England with the India ODI team, the reserve wicket-keeper of India 'A' got the scope to exhibit his potential.

And exhibit he did in splendour and style. His fearless, powerful, attacking batsmanship had not only the opposition but his own mates as well in awe. The sheer power of his strokes has had few parallels. This was not lost on the coach, Sandeep Patil, just as the talent spotters had observed and the junior selectors had concurred. By the end of the year the name of MS Dhoni was an obvious choice for the national team heading for Bangladesh. A man, who was ignored by all concerned people for four years, suddenly became the cynosure of all eyes within four months!

Which fiction writer would dare to pen such lines? No wonder it is said that truth is stranger than fiction.

Popular Legends

Syed Mushtaq Ali (1914–2005)

The first time I saw Syed Mushtaq Ali was at the Eden Gardens in the "Defence Fund Match", which was held following the India-China war in 1962. At the time in the early 1960s, Mushtaq Ali was nearing 50 and most certainly was out of cricket for more than a decade.

In our childhood days, I had heard of Mushtaq Ali's magnificent exploits from my father and uncle Tarun, who used to play club cricket in Calcutta. They would mention how he would step out of his crease to even fast bowlers and glance or cut with ease. That was supposed to be his trademark stroke.

Syed Mushtaq Ali

To be honest, it was difficult to believe that such a stroke was possible. Why should a batsman step out to a fast bowler? And even if he did, why would he do so to glance or cut the ball? It just did not make sense. It sounded incredible. I used to think that since my father and uncle belonged to Mushtaq Ali's generation, they were merely exaggerating the hero worship of their idol.

Now, I was watching the 50-year-old former opener against the fastest bowler in the world at the time, Roy Gilchrist of West Indies! A fast bowler of immense pace and ferocious nature. As Gilchrist, arms flailing, thundered in to deliver, Mushtaq Ali actually stepped out of his crease! He must have stepped out at least two yards!

Gilchrist, flabbergasted, did not release the ball. He ran down the pitch to Mushtaq Ali's end, glared at him for a while and made a sign of the cross on Mushtaq Ali, as if marking the target before turning back to bowl the next ball. Mushtaq Ali merely smiled and made a gesture of flicking a speck of dirt from his fluttering silk shirt.

The whole episode was the height of showmanship. But this was no theatre. A spark had been ignited between the world's fastest bowler and the world's most adventurous batsman. The stark reality of antagonism was palpable. The crowd was on the edge of their seats. We realized that there would be no quarters given; certainly, none asked for. The intervening moment throbbed with excitement: a fuming Gilchrist walking back to the top of his distant bowling mark; and Mushtaq, nonchalant and graceful, leaning on his bat for support.

The next ball from the fearsome Gilchrist scorched the earth but the old man was again out of his crease in no time and flicked the rising delivery off his chest over square leg to the fence. It was a combination of raw courage, superlative co-ordination of hand and eye and sense of adventure.

I had seen enough. Realised there and then, the reason why my father's generation of cricket lovers idolized Mushtaq Ali. He was not only a marvellous batsman, full of strokes and audacious nature. No, no, he was much more. For him cricket was not only a game, but an adventure. An adventure to be enjoyed and to be lived to the full.

If the adventure did not end in glory, there was no failure involved. It was just a matter of challenge. It was the sense of attempting the impossible that set him apart from others. Never before or since has a batsman stepped out to the fastest of bowlers to cut the ball or to glance or to flick. None would dare because of the physical risk involved. In fact, that was precisely the reason why Mushtaq Ali patented that stroke of his: because it was difficult to execute and because it was risky even if executed properly.

In the 1970s, I played against his son Gulrez Ali in a Duleep Trophy match at Jaipur. He had his father's easy bearing, relaxed smile and cultured manner. There, however, the comparison ended because there could not be another graceful and gracious Mushtaq Ali, not even among his own progeny.

In 1993 Mushtaq Ali had come to Calcutta at the invitation of the Voluntary Blood Donors' Association to meet the blood donors at Eden Gardens, of whom I happened to be one. I had taken a copy of his autobiography *Cricket Delightful* and requested him for his signature. Flashing a wide smile, he put down his signature and said, "Hope one day you play for India." It was very embarrassing and so I told him, "Sir, I am 43 and have given up active cricket more than a decade back."

Without any hesitation he smiled again, "You never know. They might call you for some Veterans XI." Believe it or not, by the end of that year I was actually in the India Veterans team to play against the touring Pakistanis led by Majid Khan.

After the blood donation camp was over, I invited Mushtaq Ali to the CAB indoor stadium to meet the Bengal Under-16 team members, who were my trainees. There before we could even request him, he volunteered to bat! He was nearing 80 at the time. Still ramrod straight and without an iota of excess fat, his statuesque bearing evoked instant admiration. Most of the bats he found rather heavy, as contemporary bats were. Finally, he picked up a comparatively light bat and was ready to face the bowling without any protective gear.

Syed Mushtaq Ali coming out to bat with Vijay Merchant

I asked an off-spinner to bowl. Again, he stepped out of his crease and this time he late-cut the ball with immaculate timing!

It was not the rapier thrust of a cut. No, it was a whipping action of steely wrists. Simply amazing the stroke was. At the age of 80 in totally alien conditions how did he manage to 'time' the ball is beyond my comprehension. But he did it. We saw it and were mesmerized. Never before had he played under artificial lights. Never before had he played on artificial surface. Yet he revealed to us what genius really was.

Later, I requested him to advise me and my trainees. The modest man said, "My philosophy is enjoy your cricket and give enjoyment to others. I have nothing else to say." It was brilliant. Just brilliant. In a nut-shell, he told us what sport was all about.

Mushtaq Ali's contribution to cricket and cricketers can never be judged by statistical facts and figures. He belonged to a different genre. A breed that evoked passionate love for the game among cricket followers. The top two of the rare breeds most certainly would be Keith Miller and Mushtaq Ali. They risked their fame and fortune to give entertainment to generations of cricket lovers. They never cared for statistics although their talents achieved phenomenal popularity.

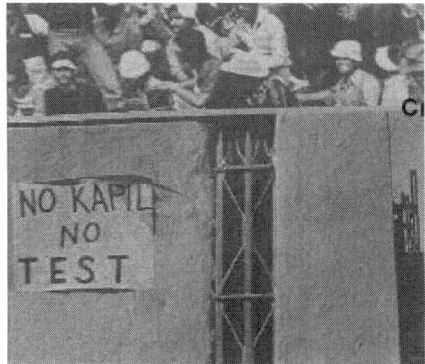

Cricket lovers from Kolkata protested the same way for Kapil Dev's exclusion in the 1984 Test against England at Eden Gardens just like the way they did for Mushtaq Ali in 1945

Both Miller and Mushtaq share a rare platform. They were brought back into the national side by the direct intervention of cricket lovers. Keith Miller, at the time the leading all-rounder of the world, was dropped by the Australian selectors which included Sir Don, from the South African tour of 1949–50. The press and public outcry at the injustice reverberated all over the world, particularly in Australia. Later the Australian selectors had to bow down to public opinion and reinstate him when one player, Bill Johnston, was injured during the tour.

So, with Mushtaq Ali. More than 70 years ago, in 1945, at Calcutta he was dropped by the national selectors, one of whom was Duleepsinhji. The emotional Bengalees were up in arms. They demonstrated in front of Eden Gardens holding placards proclaiming: "No Mushtaq, no Test". This was against Hasset's Australian Services team in 1945. Mushtaq Ali was promptly brought back to his rightful position in the XI.

This was indeed unique. Never before or since in the annals of cricket have we had a player brought back into the playing XI because of public outcry. Such was the love and admiration that cricket lovers had for the magnificent man.

Salim Durani (1934–)

When Afghanistani players take part in Test cricket as a full member nation under the aegis of International Cricket Council (ICC), they take heart that the person who took India to the top of the cricketing world for the first time ever was a man born in Afghanistan to Afghan parents.

Salim Durani

The Kabul-born Salim Aziz Durani's greatest contribution to cricket seems to have come nearly 50 years after he left the scene. The sons of the soil of the land where he was born would be stepping into his shoes as Test cricketers.

With such an inspiring role-model to follow, the future of generations of Afghanistani cricketers would do well to remember that it was one of their own cricketing grandfathers who showed the world what the Afghan blood was capable of. None other than Salim Durani was the chief contributor who made India the top cricketing nation of the world for the first time ever in 1971.

Although some people wish to say that the turning point of Indian cricket was in 1983 because India had won the ODI world cup for the first time that year, the truth is that the most significant year in Indian cricket was 1971 when India defeated West Indies and England in successive Test series within months on their own backyards. Never again could India repeat such major victories abroad within such a short term. As England had just registered a victory over Australia, India was justifiably the number one cricketing nation at a time when 'rankings' were unheard of.

The man who took India to the top of the world in 1971 happened to be the *Kabuliwala* who was christened 'Prince Salim' by his innumerable fans around the country. In 1971 at Port of Spain in Trinidad Oval as he went left-arm over the wicket, he went over the mighty West Indies batting challenge. Off two successive deliveries he ensured that Lloyd and Sobers were back in the pavilion taking off their pads. The artist in him gave a soft smile as he twirled his magical fingers and closed his eyes for a moment to thank Allah for His blessing.

Salim Durani

West Indies never quite recovered from the embarrassment and crashed to a humiliating defeat to Ajit Wadekar's Indians. One young debutant by the name of Sunil Manohar Gavaskar scored two half centuries at Trinidad to begin a career that helped Indians to walk twenty feet tall in the cricket firmament. India went on to win the series against a team that had the likes of Rohan Kanhai, Garfield Sobers, Roy Fredricks and Clive Lloyd.

Believe it or not, Salim Durani was omitted within months from the following tour to England in 1971! The man, who had helped India to win against the all-conquering West Indies for the first time – that too on their soil – was dropped within 3 months of that historic victory. So very typical of the weird thought-process of our national selectors, whom Mohinder Amarnath once described as a 'bunch of jokers'.

Salim Durani showed no emotion. He had become used to this unjust treatment from petty people around him. People biased and short-sighted were sitting on judgment on a genius. Salim was born at a wrong time, in a wrong country. Never received the recognition due to him from the cricket administrators of the country he was bred at.

Salim Durani was a free soul without a care for the morrow. Had no inhibition; had no ego. He borrowed money and bought beer and coke to share with the 'creditor'! Next day in the subtlest manner possible, he left the exact amount into the man's shirt pocket! I can vouch for the incident because the person happened to be me. At Hyderabad during the Moin-ud-Dowla Trophy way back in 1976.

In a career that spanned nearly 15 years, the magnificent all-rounder played in only 29 Tests. He went on two tours only – both to the Caribbean ten years apart – where he showed the world his true greatness. The national selectors, in all their wisdom, realized that Durani would be a 'passenger' on tours to England, Australia and New Zealand between 1959 and 1974! The overseas performance of the India team during that period, rather not be described and dissected.

Once I asked him the reason for being was omitted from the Indian team to England in 1967. The disarming smile softly uttered, "The selectors thought England would be too cold for me." Why not to Australia and New Zealand the following year? A subtle wink elaborated, "May be too hot for me."

In 1961–62 when India won a series against England for the first time, the chief architects were the all-round skills of Salim Aziz Durani and Chandrakant Gulabrao Borde. At Eden Gardens, Salim Durani had Ted Dexter and Ken Barrington in no end of trouble with 8 wickets in India's victory.

In the following Test at Madras another Indian victory was possible because of the magnificent all-rounder's 10-wicket haul.

Salim Durani

Despite match-winning performances Salim Durani was never to get the recognition that he deserved from the cricket administration.

Handsome is as the handsome does, so goes the cliché. Absolutely true in Durani's case. The greenish-blue eyes looked at the world from a tall, handsome frame. He was all elegance and style. Even the glamorous world of Bollywood had to relent by offering him a hero's role opposite Parveen Babi in BR Ishara's *Charitra*. This also happens to be another 'first' of his among Indian Test cricketers.

In 1962 when no one quite wanted to face the fiery Wesley Hall on those lightning-fast, hard West Indies pitches of the time, it was this man who volunteered to bat at number 3! And, for good measure, scored a magnificent century against the likes of Sobers, Gibbs and Hall. Surely, he did not mean to offend anyone, but the brave century knock did embarrass the prima donna batters no end. Not that it mattered to him. He was just doing something that came naturally to him.

Salim Durani was born according to conscientious researcher and brilliant analyst Gulu Ezekiel on a train moving towards Kabul in 1934 at a time when his father, Abdul Aziz, was keeping wickets for the Nawanagar State team in pre-independent India. After India's independence in 1947, Aziz went to Pakistan, but Aziz's his family settled down in the newly formed State of Gujarat. Destiny had decreed that Durani would be Afghan by birth but Indian by nationality, as was the case with millions of others affected by the disastrous partition of the sub-continent.

He was the people's man. A hero to millions. At Calcutta people still – nearly 50 years since he last played for India – go crazy when they see him. When my book on the 150th year of Eden Gardens was in print, a cricket addict said, "I shall buy the book only if Durani's photo is on the cover. No one ever was more popular than he at Eden." Absolutely correct was he.

In 1972 the highly voluble crowd at the erstwhile Ranji Stadium structure asked for a 'sixer'. Durani actually waved at them and, believe it or not, put the next delivery from Derek Underwood right into the upper tier! That is the heroic appeal he had.

In 2014 the Additional Solicitor-General of India, Bishwajit Bhattacharyya, flew down from New Delhi to meet his boyhood hero at the Nagaraj bar of the hallowed Bengal Club in Kolkata. This is the kind of exceptional popularity our Salim-bhai still commands.

He always seemed to keep his best for the Eden Gardens crowd. In 1965 in one over of magic weave he had three Aussies in hypnosis. Unfortunately, his wonderful spell did not get the acknowledgement as the match was curtailed owing to unseasonal rain. "Yes, I enjoyed the support of the crowd at Eden. To be honest, I enjoy only if the spectators enjoy wherever that be. Otherwise what is the purpose of sports?" How true. Only a genuine artist like Prince Salim can say so in such an easy, relaxed manner.

His charm was captivating. Once in a Duleep Trophy tie, the bowler Durani actually applauded a cover-driven boundary of mine! I was too stunned to react. It took me moments to realize the fathomless magnanimity of the man.

His simplicity, his modesty, his love for life and his love for companionship are lessons to learn from. Once In 2014 at the inauguration ceremony of my book *Eden Gardens: Legend & Romance* he told a packed audience at Eden Gardens, "...I always wanted to be a railway engine driver... Never thought I had any talent for cricket...Life has been good to me...No regrets at all..."

Only a man of Salim Aziz Durani's class can say so despite all the injustices that he had to bear over the decades. So casual and unconcerned was the man about his own well-being that he even would not go to collect the honorarium some benefactor in Bombay had decided to give him on a monthly basis!

Seema with author's favourite cricketer

Never once has anyone heard him criticize another person. Not even a harsh word passed through his lips. That was quite beyond him. He believed in enjoyment. He enjoyed his life, his cricket. And in return he gave far more enjoyment to others, whether they were spectators or friends. Doubt if he ever had a foe. A man of few words, when he spoke his soft, chaste voice was all music. He was and still remains, the Prince Charming of Indian cricket.

Great cricketers would be born again and again. But there will never be another to match this nonchalant, selfless genius.

Gundappa Vishwanath (1949–)

The unique appeal of Vishy was the universal admiration for him. No other cricketer received the kind of adulation that he received from his opponents, peers and competitors alike. No one seemed to have had an altercation with him. No one can remember any misdemeanour on his part. None has ever said a word against him. No malice. As peers, we were mesmerized by his genius.

His is a unique place in the annals of cricket. As an artist he was supreme. His sportsmanship traversed all obstacles. His wit had class and subtlety. He was not tall, lean or born with chiselled features. Nothing in his exterior form suggested that

Gundappa Vishwanath

he was extraordinary. Yet that was exactly what he was and precisely where he scored above all others. Whatever he did, he did effortlessly. Whenever he spoke, it was all humour and civil. When he batted he made the difficult art of batting look easy.

Vishy's muscular forearms and wrists of steel we envied. Once I asked him the secret, as he never appeared to do any physical exercise. Very coolly, he picked up an empty beer glass and repeatedly brought the glass to his lips and lowered it again! He smiled, "Raju, if you do this often enough, you too will have similar forearms and wrists!" Instantly he slapped my right palm in his famous trademark style of appreciation. That's Gundappa for you.

Highly impressive though his statistical record is, the 6080 runs that he sketched for India was merely incidental. Most certainly not his major contribution. The essence of his contribution were the innumerable match-winning innings, the courageous fight-backs in defence of India's honour and, most significantly, the endless hours of pristine pleasure that he distributed to cricket lovers the world over with his charming style and manner.

Yet his initiation into international cricket had neither charm nor grace. As the young debutant walked back with a nought against his name, a team-mate remarked, "Why have these fancy types when we have hardened ones available." In the 2nd essay, an innings of infinite charm and variety unfolded. Wristy cuts and flicks fetched 25 boundaries in a score of 137. Sheer timing and artistry captivated the Kanpur crowd. Skipper Mansur Ali Khan Pataudi asked the senior man to take back his words.

Gundappa Vishwanath

In the following Test at Delhi he helped India to register a resounding victory against the likes of Graham McKenzie and Ashley Mallet. Those who had come to snigger now went back singing praises. There was an ethereal beauty in whatever he did. The cricket field was his canvas where he etched a rare form of art.

Even today, decades after his retirement I have seen people shed tears of joy in recounting his greatness. And why not? How can they forget the small, lean frame walking out to meet the Goliaths at Eden Gardens on a murky morning in 1969? India was tottering at 2 wickets down for zero, with the Aussies breathing fire. Unruffled he appeared like a kid who did not know that he had walked into a lion's den.

Not a soul stirred as he took his relaxed stance. The environment had all the sinister forebodings: innings collapsing, gloomy surroundings, Aussie slang, pitch tinged with green and freshly laden with dew. Even the Biblical David could not possibly have had such odds stacked against him. The first two deliveries were coaxed to the fence on either side of the brilliant cover-point Paul Sheahan. Thunderous applause broke loose. Ninety thousand Calcuttans realized the presence of a genius. They stood up in respect: Shiva's own creation was in action.

Gundappa Raghunath Vishwanath was to enact numerous such sterling innings of character and artistry the world over. But exactly where would he be in the pantheon of batsmanship? His consistency never matched Sir Don's output. Nor did he possess the technical acumen of Sir Jack Hobbs or Hanif Mohammed. Neither the glamour of Denis Compton or Sir Gary Sobers. Nor did he acquire the power of Vivian Richards or the mammoth achievements of Sunil Gavaskar. Then how would he be evaluated?

When serious cricket addicts discuss Vishy they do not waste time with his statistical record, impressive though those are. Mere figures cannot tell the story of his artistry. Words fail to picture his actual worth. No turn of phrase seems adequate. He needed a Tagore or a Shakespeare to do justice to his talents. He was in a surreal world of his own: giving pleasure to others as much he derived enjoyment from the game.

He did not belong to the materialistic age of ours. His batsmanship was not a thought but a feeling. Vishy took us to rarefied realms. He had every orthodox stroke in his repertoire, but he executed them in his own unique way. Made batting appear to be the easiest of pastimes! For him to cut or flick from the stumps, that too against the movement, was as simple as dipping an *idli* into *sambar*. He never seemed to lose his composure, his balance or his natural elegance.

Sunil Gavaskar is on record that no other batsman seemed as set from the first delivery as Vishy did. The fearsome West Indies fast bowlers of the 1970s agreed that of all the batsmen, he was the most authoritative against them. Players far and wide, mates and opponents, were unanimous in their love for him. His charm and artistry captivated his peers as much as it the connoisseurs. He was one in a million. Never stooped to gamesmanship or the so-called 'killer instinct' to thrive in the heat of battle.

Vishwanath performed beautifully wherever he played the game. Was the first Indian to score centuries against every Test playing country at home and abroad. He was comfortable to pace and spin alike. One of his finest exhibitions was against Clive Lloyd's West Indies at Eden Gardens in 1974. A flawless innings of 139 unfolded which laid the foundation of a grand victory as Chandrasekhar drove the final nails on the last day. A scintillating innings of 97 not out enabled India to win the following Test at Chennai.

Away from India too, he was his relaxed self. On that fateful day at Port of Spain in 1976 when the West Indies fast bowlers were peppering the Indians with bouncers, characteristically little Gundappa revealed his courage as his century helped India to record a historic victory, by chasing more than 400 runs. One pertinent point of Vishy's batting was that he scored his centuries so rapidly that it allowed the bowlers enough time to run through the opposition.

Sunil Gavaskar and Gundappa Vishwanath

He held 63 catches in his 91 Tests, 87 of which were consecutive. His Test average is as high as 41.93 and includes 14 centuries with 222 as his highest score. Excellent though his figures are, still those miserably fail to do justice to this noble cricketer.

Such was his spirit that once he even called back a batsman on being given out. At Mumbai in the BCCI's Jubilee Test against England in 1980, Vishwanath led India. When Bob Taylor was given out caught behind, the batsman told Vishy that he had not touched the ball. Promptly Vishy informed the umpire that he was withdrawing the appeal! Taylor and Botham added vital runs and India lost the match. Without Vishy's generosity, the great soul that he was, England would not have won the match.

He of course became the target of criticism from all quarters. Even lost his captaincy. But he did not show any regret, any remorse. Merely smiled his misfortune away. Forever the artist, he never bothered to change his style or his attitude to the game. Never fretted or fumed about criticisms or conditions. Never gave a thought to fame or fortune. He was a singular man in his approach. Far, far removed from the humdrum world of mortal men and their rat races.

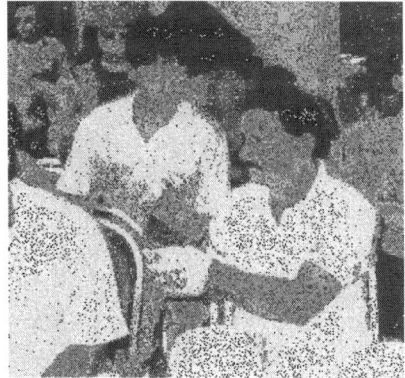

Calcutta's perpetual favourite: author's son Tej with his hero at CC&FC

Yet at the same time he was a man of the world. A lover of life. A man of remarkable wit. He saw humour in the gravest of crises. Once in a Ranji Trophy tie when an umpire negated an appeal against him, the suffering bowler Subroto Guha suggested, "That was a straight ball." Immediately a smile surfaced on Vishy's face, "Bacchu (Guha's nickname), marvellous swinger that you are, the ball must have been swinging away."

When people applauded, little Vishy would modestly doff his cap and raise his bat all-round the ground to acknowledge. Not for him the rudeness of pointing the bat at some particular people. Such crassness never engulfed him. Our idol Gundappa symbolized the sentiment that it is not the school but the schooling that makes a man.

Artistry is in the eyes and ears of subtle minds. Connoisseurs regarded Vishwanath a genius. An artist with the sitar of a bat. He played mellow tunes with the willow. Sending his audiences to ethereal heights. His saintly demeanour evoked admiration, respect and love. Only a genius could make the people respond so. In the cricketing pantheon, Gundappa Vishwanath is the Shiva: a noble head and a noble heart.

Rebels

Probir "Khokon" Sen (1926–1970)

Today if one walks into the CAB club house at Eden Gardens, one would come across a wall in the central lounge where a list of Test players from Bengal appears. The list begins with a glaring error. The first name itself is wrong! Just goes to show how much of pride and interest we have in our own selves! Of course, there are a whole lot of other wrong names in that list, as well.

Probir Kumar Sen (Khokon)

Over the last 15 years the list with the embarrassing errors has stayed on despite repeated requests to alter. No CAB president, neither Jagmohan Dalmiya nor Sourav Ganguly, has shown any interest in having the list rectified. Complete ignorance? Or, sheer indifference? Dalmiya once defended, "The names on the lists were as guided by a foreign-returned cricket-scholar!"

Unfortunately, even an erudite man like Sunil Gavaskar fell into the trap and once commented in his television broadcast that the first Bengali Test player was Shute Banerjee! Sunil of course was relying on the piece of information available to him in the official site of CAB. Shute Banerjee's name is prominently displayed on the CAB lounge to mislead the whole world.

Shute Banerjee was representing Bihar, and not Bengal, when he made his Test debut for India in 1948–49 at Bombay in the 5th and final Test of the series.

The first Bengali player to play for India was not Shute Banerjee, but Probir Kumar Sen, popularly known as Khokon. In 1947–48 he went with skipper Lala Amarnath's team to Australia as the second wicket-keeper to Jamshed Irani. But after two Tests the team management realized that they had made a blunder by omitting Sen from the first XI.

Just out of teens, Khokon Sen brought about a radical change in the ethos of Indian cricketers. Joking, chatting, playing pranks, the vivacious youngster injected some fresh air in the claustrophobic ambience of Indian cricket. He was not a rebel in the conventional sense. He was not fighting for any cause. He was just himself: extrovert, entertainer, energy personified.

Probir Sen standing 2nd from left with the 1952 Indian cricket team in England

Perpetually on the move, he seemed to be. Came into national reckoning by his superlative talents. He had no Dutta Ray or Dalmiya to plead for him. He was an independent individual who cared little about what others felt about him. Not a respecter of persons or things, he maintained his originality in every step of his. He did not join groups, nor did he fall for any 'carrots' dangled. He maintained his composure, come rain, hail or sunshine.

Khokon Sen's career was a massive mass of misunderstanding. People enjoyed his company but ridiculed him behind his back. He was always thought to be pompous because of his very close rapport with royalty. Actually, he was an extrovert with the softest of souls. Just as he was close to the maharajas so was he to the masseurs.

Khokonda nicknamed Jeevan Paul, the humble masseur of the Bengal team, 'Stanley' after the famous publisher of cricket books, Stanley Paul. He was as comfortable with 'Bhaya', the Maharaja of Cooch Behar.

The Maharaja of Cooch Behar, Jagaddipendra Narayan Bhup Bahadur, who was very popular as 'Bhaya', was an elder brother to Khokonda. They were very thick friends on and off the field. Bhaya captained Bengal in the Ranji Trophy in the 1940s while Probir Sen took over in the following decade.

Khokonda's hearty laughter was as appealing as his big heart. Hailing from a wealthy family, the generous persona loved having people around him to relax and regale. With Bhaya, he would be seen at social clubs, palaces, angling expeditions and shikars. He enjoyed the best of liquor and was voracious with Continental cuisine, particularly crabs and prawns, but made no effort to feel defensive about either.

Unfortunately, his gregarious nature, his easy laughter, his practical jokes were thought to be of a man yet to mature. His Bengal team mates which included Nirmal Chatterjee (Bengal's best-ever all-round sportsman) and Badal Dutta (Bengal captain and Cambridge University Blue) as well as the Test cricketer Montu Banerjee loved and adored him. Even the great Indian contemporaries like Vinoo Mankad, Vijay Hazare and Polly Umrigar found him to be excellent company. The fashionable man would wear Barkat Ali suits with felt hats tilted stylishly. Those were the days...

But generally, the cricketing community, particularly the officials, found his ever-cheerful nature reprehensible. For them an ideal sportsman was expected to be a teetotaller, a person who would not talk or contradict, a person who would perpetually kowtow to officials. Khokonda most surely did not quite fulfil the criteria and thankfully never bothered to. In fact, he was exactly at the opposite end. Ultimately his cheerful nature became a noose, but little did he care.

Sen, barely 20 at the time, began at Melbourne and was an instant success with his wicket-keeping. Brilliantly acrobatic, he was an extrovert character who just could not keep quiet. He would chatter constantly from behind the wicket with the fieldsmen and the bowlers.

He would liven up a dreary, boring afternoon on the field with his incessant fund of stories.

His exceptional wicket-keeping ability came into focus during the War years when first-class cricket continued in India. He made his Ranji Trophy debut for Bengal in 1943–44 and received high acclaim from all quarters. Born in 1927 at Comilla (now in Bangladesh), Khokon Sen showed exceptional promise as an all-round sportsman from his school days.

His contemporaries found the young man – full of humour and highly pro-active – a delight. His child-like simplicity attracted attention. He was full of pranks even in State-level matches. He was always doing the unexpected. Not an 'opener', he opened the innings and got a century in Ranji Trophy.

If this was not enough, once he took off his gloves and began to bowl. The umpire asked, "Over-the-wicket? Or, round?" The instant answer was, "Sir, from beside the wicket, if you do not mind." Believe it or not, he actually has a hat-trick in Ranji

From left: Don Bradman, Pankaj Gupta, Jessie Bradman and Probir Sen at the Dum Dum (Kolkata) airport lounge. This was the only time Bradman set foot on Indian soil on his way to UK with his wife in 1953

Trophy. Wonder if this is a world record for a wicket-keeper.

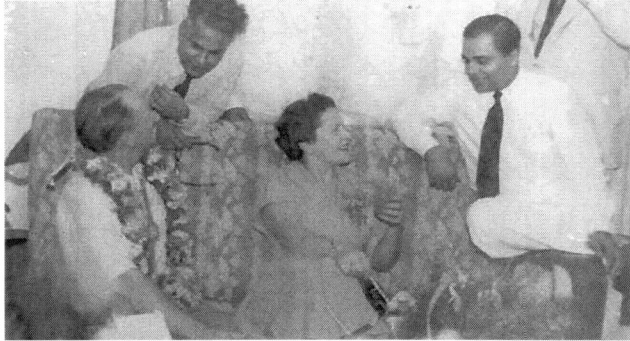

It is said that Bill Ferguson, the famous scorer, once told Sen that he reminded him of the England wicket-keeper George Duckworth who also had the habit of constant chatter. Sen turned around and told him, "I don't just talk and talk. I guide. I give encouragement." And then in

his typical camaraderie embraced Ferguson and went for a round of beer. No wonder the Indians were very popular as tourists those days.

Sen had a very happy tour on and off the field in Australia. On a disastrous tour, apart from Hazare, Mankad and to an extent Dattu Phadkar, the youngest member Sen was an outstanding success. Being a superb social-mixer, he became the toast of the evenings when the Indians would spend a lot of time with Don Bradman for advice. In the match against South Australia he flashed off Bradman's bails with lightning speed on the very difficult leg-side. Bradman, true to his character, was full of praise for young stumper's speed, anticipation and agility.

On that tour of Australia, every Indian cricketer was offered the scope to say two sentences over the long-distance phone that had just been introduced between India and Australia. Almost all the players said that they were fine except, of course, the one and only Khokon Sen. When his turn came, the 20-year old Khokon shouted, "Dadu, send money. Nothing left!" That was typical of him: no other message worthy enough! He endeared himself to all those who played with and against him.

Sen played for India against West Indies at home in 1948–49 then went to England in 1952 as well as was a regular in the national team at the time. Although a regular member the opportunities were sadly limited to only 14 Tests.

The highpoint of his career was the victory at Madras in 1951–52. Skipper Vijay Hazare's team defeated Nigel Howard's MCC very convincingly with Roy and Umrigar getting hundreds and Vinoo Mankad capturing 12 wickets. They were the prime architects of the victory.

But one man made headlines from an unusual position. That was Khokon Sen. He had a hand in 5 stumpings. This was exemplary wicket-keeping no doubt but what was more appealing was the man's stage-craft. One moment he would be throwing the ball up and juggling with it. Next moment he would start to roll on the ground to the cheers of the crowd. And in the very next instant he would be running around the pitch with the ball in hand like a goal-scorer in football. Sen captivated the audience and the media lapped it up. He was indeed a born showman.

I met him just once. Was the year 1970? I distinctly remember the date 26th January for many reasons than the obvious one. I was a member of the Mohun Bagan team which went to Kalighat Club ground to play an exhibition match. Our captain was the mercurial Chuni Goswami.

Just prior to the match, our dressing room vibrated with the laughter of a diminutive, stocky man of around 45. Unmistakably Khokon Sen. He was cracking jokes with Chunida, Shyamuda and my elder brother Deb when his eyes fell on me. "Who's this?" he furrowed his eyebrows. Someone mentioned, "Deb's younger brother." "Deb's brother?" he fumed, "Unshaven? You must try to look like a cricketer."

Like most precocious college youth, I had little respect for persons who had no time for me. I coolly uttered, "Sir, have you not heard of

Probir Sen shaking hands with Queen Elizabeth II.
Other players from left: Vijay Hazare (captain), Pankaj Gupta (manager), Hemu Adhikari, Vinoo Mankad, Chandu Sarwate, Dattu Phadkar and Pankaj Roy

WG Grace?" There was pin-drop silence. Stunned, Khokonda instantly recovered, smiled, put his hand on my shoulder, "Son, why hide your handsome face with a beard?" I forced a smile in return. As Khokonda left our room, my brother was furious with me for my silly response. Little did we realize that the famous man had come to take an active part in that 'friendly' fixture. He had come in cream flannels and had his India blazer on. He was well past his prime and had not played at all for over a decade. Why did he decide to play that particular match will forever be a question that would go unanswered?

Next afternoon we heard that Khokonda was no more. After the match he had some spurious rum that burnt his gullet. What a dreadful death for a cheerful man. I happened to be his last victim as a wicket-keeper. He held my 'edge' – a simple, straight forward catch – and then leaned to his right, allowed the body to fall gently and roll over in front of second slip! For ever a showman. A lovable joker. A wonderful human being.

I have the highest regard for him because he was a true sportsman: modest, humorous, determined, chivalrous and highly talented. Khokonda was incapable of hurting anyone. A man who had given endless hours of mirth to all around him. For Khokon Sen, sport did not mean keeping officials and influential people happy. Not being an employee of any princely family, he mixed with them at par socially. Did not suffer from any complex. Most certainly a revolutionary departure from the routine in the 1930s and 1940s.

His approach to life revolutionized cricket in India to a great extent. It is not commonly realized that this man of wit was a messenger of life-style. He was like Charlie Chaplin the immortal of the film world: humour laced with message. To bring about changes he did not fight with anyone. Through his child-like simplicity he made others realize their folly. Back-stabbing, conspiracies, groupism, loose-talk, parochialism, etcetera which had inundated Indian cricket at the time gradually became severely restricted.

He brought about a silent revolution in Indian cricket with his characteristic sense of humour. He was not a rebel with a whole lot of causes. His rebellion was one of approach. Through personal example, he planted the idea of enjoyment among Indian players: sport was meant to be enjoyed; sport was for providing entertainment to others; sport was a delightful means to camaraderie; sport was life to be lived.

The charming rebel of Indian cricket left us at 45, much too early. It is said... those whom the gods love, leave young...

Bishen Singh Bedi (1946–)

On a crisp December morning at Eden Gardens as a 22-year old Amritsar-born Sikh went over-the-wicket, he went over the next generation of left-arm orthodox Indian spinners. Frail of physique but fearless at heart he teased and tormented the might of Sobers' West Indies batters. The aerial curve of the flight trajectory was not a tossed-up delivery but an arc of deception. He was a spin bowler who actually could turn the ball on any surface and under any condition.

Bishen Singh Bedi

Bishen Bedi was and remains a pioneer in many respects. He was the first among Indians to come from an unfancied city to become an international cricket legend. He was the first to break the stranglehold of Bombay who monopolized the domestic Indian cricket championships. He was most surely the first in northern India to help the deserving regional youngsters to find their feet in the uncertain world of Indian cricket. He was the first among our national selectors who had the courage to identify and select 'horses for courses' when it came to choosing the national teams. And most importantly he was the first to vehemently protest at the international stage when the game of cricket was reduced to a street-fight.

However, all these impeccable qualities do little justice to this ubiquitous personality. Unique though those attributes were, he was primarily an artiste. As with all genuine people of art he was a philosopher and a social activist. When Swami Vivekananda mentioned that it was more important to take part in active sports than to sit in passive prayer, the saint had the vision of Bishen Bedi in mind. For the highly principled man it was the sincere, honest effort above all else, and certainly not the ultimate result that mattered. He happens to be the ultimate *Karma-yogi*.

Like all seers Bishen knew too well that the final result in not in human hands: only recourse men have is on the effort. No man can guarantee success in any sphere of life. Again, to take a leaf of Swamiji's teachings, Bishen too believed that the means to an end was as important as the result. This he proved at Sahiwal as well at Kingston when he vigorously protested that the spirit of cricket was being tarnished. Even Bishen's critics will admit that the turbaned Sikh had tremendous faith in himself. His confidence level and the sense of self-respect were exemplary. Invariably enough, he was always fighting for a selfless cause, however difficult it might appear to be.

In his prime Indian cricket meant Bombay and Bombay. Most deservingly because Bombay were the undisputed champions for decades. No one doubted their superiority. But Bishen wanted to halt the monopoly. This he achieved almost single-handedly by identifying and nurturing the young talents around him. He injected confidence in them, motivated them through actions and words and ultimately achieved to upset Bombay's domination in no uncertain manner.

During the course of his life's journey, he trod on many toes. Powerful, influential ones. But he had no regrets. Never cared for useless tact or external support. Never bothered about who or how many were with him. He was always a singular man with a definite purpose. His best quality was that he could be your dearest friend and at the same time your prime adversary. Depending totally on the issue at hand. This sterling quality comes only to a very few. Thankfully Bishen had loads of it. This was the characteristic that kept him apart from most others.

Magnanimous to a fault, Bishen had the knack of applauding an opponent for an exquisite stroke, even off his own bowling. I can vouch as a recipient. He was known to go across to the opponent's dressing room for a chat. These came naturally to him for he enjoyed companionship.

Never seen him lower his high moral code to take an undue advantage, even if it was legal and available. Never seen him lose his cool and composure on the field. Never saw him lose his dignity. But he would be the first to object if he found any wrong being done. Tony Greig and John Lever got a taste of his medicine in 1976 when they were illegally applying artificial substance to the ball. Bishen was forever a patriot. The so-called professionalism of the mercenary never crossed his mind as Northamptonshire CC cut short his contract because of this incident.

India's first series victory in 1969 was not taken seriously because New Zealand was considered to be a weak opposition. But under 'home' conditions the Kiwis were a formidable lot. Tiger Pataudi's men did wonders with Bedi and Prasanna among the principal wicket-takers. A major turning point of Indian cricket was the twin overseas victories of Wadekar's men in West Indies and England in 1971. Bishen was a prominent contributor on both tours.

Even after retirement, his contribution was impeccable. Bedi took the initiative to be the chief architect who chose the 1983 world cup squad. For the first time India sent a team with the 'horses for courses' policy. Brilliant fielders, genuine swingers, lion-hearted batters brought forth a stunning result beyond all comprehension. Salute to our national selectors where Bishen along with Chandu Borde and Ghulam Ahmed played a very prominent role for their unbiased, non-provincial approach. The appointment of Maan Singh as manager was a masterstroke as Maan's personality and integrity played a crucial role during the campaign.

Bishen Bedi was born 50 years too late. His ideologies, his mannerisms, his conduct were of an earlier generation when values had some value. He was a complete misfit of his contemporary times and beyond. He was aghast at the dreadful cronyism and the hypocrisy around him. Frustrated, he could not afford to keep silent. He became a rebel because of the prevailing circumstances; not because he loved rebellion. It was his unique protests during international encounters against West Indies at Kingston in 1976 and against Pakistan at Sahiwal in 1978 that coerced MCC – years later – to bring about the page on 'spirit of cricket' to precede the laws of cricket. Thankfully all over the cricket world the concept of 'spirit of cricket' became the guiding pole-star. But the man who rebelled and forced the change never got his recognition. Not that he cared. That is the ultimate beauty of this selfless soul.

The Northern Punjab debutant first saw Test cricket in the first Test match he played. His baptism was literally in flames. He saw first-hand how a cricket-loving crowd could flare up and give the Establishment a run for its life. When on 1st January 'daily' tickets were sold far in excess of the ground capacity in the erstwhile Ranji Block, true to tradition the Eden Gardens cricket followers from every section of the ground erupted in anger. Cricket lovers chased the inefficient police and thrashed the corrupt officials to vent their feelings. It was a lesson not to be forgotten. Later when Bishen fought officialdom and peers he knew that there was nothing to fear about when one fought for the correct cause. Justice exists nowhere; nor did Bishen ever find it.

Very few are blessed to appreciate fine art. Fine art is most certainly a subjective matter. Cannot be calculated, measured or weighed. It is in the eyes,

The author with Michael Holding, Chuni Goswami, BS Chandrasekhar and Bishen Singh Bedi during the release of his book: Eden Gardens – Legend & Romance

ears and mind of the beholder. How would you evaluate Leonardo da Vinci or Michelangelo? How would one compare Mohammed Rafi to Kishore Kumar? Is it possible to calculate the contributions of authors and actors? The moment we try to bring in material tools of evaluation we do an injustice to the concept of fine art.

This has been a perpetual problem in Indian sport. We are forever counting runs and wickets; averages and aggregates; appearances and goals. Little do we realize that all such figures will evaporate in future. In time someone else with more opportunities, better equipment, easier conditions, different techniques, and wider media publicity will overtake the earlier performers. Does it mean that Ranji and Bradman, O'Reilly and Larwood were inferior to the post-war and modern-day stars?

Every era would produce its champions. A genuine champion of one era would also be a genuine champion of another era if that was possible. These hypothetical comparisons are odious and do serious injustice to the former greats. Unfortunately, Bishen Bedi and players of his artistic ilk have always been judged on calculators. Although Bishen's statistical figures are of the highest category contributing towards many distinguished Test victories, yet it is primarily his artistic talents that have delighted generations of cricket connoisseurs. He was and remains the antidote to the art of tactfulness. He himself would be the first to admit that he was not born to be a diplomat. If anything, he was what was said of Rousseau: "whatever touched his heart, unloosened his tongue". Admittedly over the years, Bishen Bedi has paid a heavy penalty for this quality of his. But he would not have had it otherwise. Fear of authority never crossed that up-raised, proud turban of his.

Most unfortunately the media played up the subtle differences between Sunil Gavaskar and Bishen Bedi. Actually, they complemented each other as the leading towers of the modern Indian cricket super-structure, so very carefully put together by the magnificent presence of the one and only Polly Umrigar.

To Bedi's credit he had no time for prima donnas. He treated all men as equals. As a captain, he made young cricketers reach beyond themselves. He gave his wards freedom and respect. He fought tooth and nail for them. But he was a terrible judge of people. He hated flatterers and fiends but that was precisely what he eventually had beside him always. Invariably he was left stranded by the very men he had helped to find moorings.

The magical rhythm of his twinkling toes, the slow curve of his arms, the subtle wait, the trademark thumb impression on the ball of the non-bowling arm and the impassive vein gave him a halo that sent shivers of excitement to those fortunate enough to have seen him in action.

How Basil Butcher succumbed, and Clive Lloyd perished were not his concern for he was no Caesar. He was primarily an artist inside the canvas of a cricket field. There were no hurrahs, no high-fives. No need for that. The artist was content to exhibit his mastery and accepted the applause with a gentle bow and disarming smile. That was and still very much remains my Bishen Singh Bedi in excelsis...

Sunil Manohar Gavaskar (1949–)

Sunil Gavaskar is without an iota of doubt a national monument. A monument to the cause of cricket. In him culminated the long and difficult period of trials and tribulations of the ethos of Indian cricket.

He wore many hats: player, captain, freelance journalist, author of books, television commentator, committee member and, for a very short period, the 'acting' president of BCCI (Board of Control for Cricket in India) as well. Very few sports personalities can lay claim to such a wide spectrum of activities. On each and every platform he left behind an indelible imprint of his.

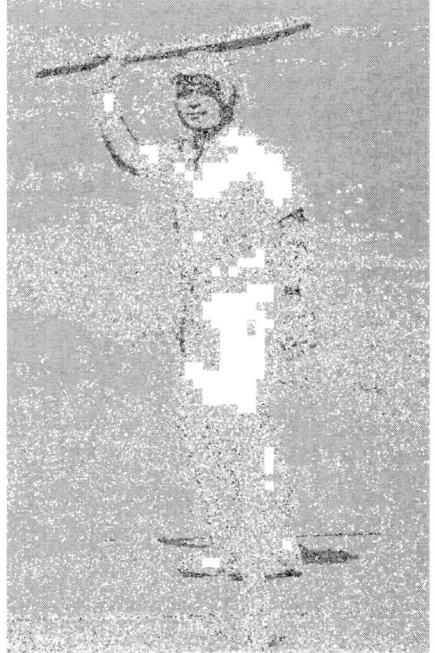

Sunil Gavaskar

Perfectionists possess self-doubts. Sincere self-doubts that lead to deep introspection. Bernard Shaw thought aloud that the truly learned had serious self-doubts. Socrates, it is believed, time and again philosophized that he had grave doubts about his own self. So, did Einstein and Shakespeare. The great Indian sages spent years in solitude reflecting and doubting, doubting and reflecting. The contemplative mind assisted them to analyse themselves. To get to 'know thyself'.

To this genre belongs Sunil Manohar Gavaskar. A man who has always been in complete control over his thoughts, words and actions.

Ever since he reeled off those endless centuries and double centuries in school and university cricket championships, he strove to learn about his own strengths and weaknesses. Soon enough he grasped that he had extraordinary potential as a cricketer. After this realization, it has been an endless climb to different peaks of achievement.

India has produced men of outstanding merit and immense genius. Men of courage, of character and of conviction. But, sad to relate, very few have reached the top-most rung in their chosen arena at the international arena. Most of our potential greats in every sphere of life have fallen on the way to their destined peaks. Some did step on the top but only for a fleeting moment. For most the pinnacle proved too steep, too slippery or, perhaps, too narrow.

Sunil Gavaskar happens to be an exceptional Indian champion in more senses than one. A supreme craftsman at work; concentration paramount; confidence in abundance; assured of his own ability. Never gave the slightest hint of losing his balance. His footmarks were permanently etched on the rock edifice of cricket. His exceptional quality was that he was perpetually trying to cross the extremity of his own wide orbit and doing so with conviction and stolidity.

Such was his strength of character that during the course of his playing days he did not refrain from criticizing influential BCCI officials. He got his message across in no uncertain terms. Once he turned down the offer of life membership to the prestigious MCC at Lord's. On numerous occasions he was vehement in criticizing the ICC. His incisive criticisms have led to many substantial improvements.

Sunil Gavaskar during his 1st tour to West Indies in 1971

First time I met him was at the Lal Bahadur Shastri Stadium at Fateh Maidan in Hyderabad. The year was 1966, the month May. About 30 young school cricketers from all over the country congregated to be fine-tuned under the supervision of former England Test cricketer TS Worthington. After the first day's session, our coach distinctly murmured, "From today I shall call you Gaviji. You will soon play for India and create records." The visionary coach used the typical Indian term of respect for an extraordinary talent. What a way to compliment.

As an active player Sunil bestrode the cricket world like a colossus. Runs he made in such mammoth proportions that he left all his contemporaries around the world way behind. Invariably comparisons with the past legends began and even the foreign correspondents very reluctantly had to concede that he was among the greatest ever. But Sunil was not content to relax with such high accolades. To him this was just one of the numerous Himalayan peaks he had decided to conquer.

On crossing the Bradmanesque barrier of Test centuries, very modestly Sunil admitted, "Mine is only an achievement because Sir Don scored his 29 Test centuries in only 80 innings." This sense of proportion; this sense of courtesy is what makes Sunil Gavaskar so different from most other champion sportsmen.

Indian schoolboy trainees at Hyderabad in 1966. SMG (front row, 4th from right), Sanjay Jagdale (back row, 4th from left), later became a prominent BCCI official, author (back row, 2nd from left). Front row, in the centre is the coach, the former England Test cricketer TS Worthington. Almost the full squad here went on to become first-class cricketers

Sunil Gavaskar's prolific performances have been delineated so frequently that further repetition would only dilute the flavour. He worked incessantly for his team, for his mates and most surely for himself. Even his greatest critic must acknowledge that every run of his 10,122 was added to India's total between 1971 and 1987.

Some have aired the notion that he did not win many matches for India. In fact, his debut scores of 65 and 67 not out at Trinidad helped India to achieve her first-ever Test and series victory over West Indies in 1971. His centuries have won Test matches at Melbourne, Auckland, Chennai and Mumbai. Innumerable times his broad bat saved India from the humiliation of defeat.

His 221 at the Oval in 1979 nearly won the Test match for India, lest it be forgotten. It is not the result that is all-important. At Thermopylae the Greeks lost but posterity salutes them for the valour shown. He and his courageous mates showed rare heroism to withstand the bouncer-bombardment at Kingston in 1976.

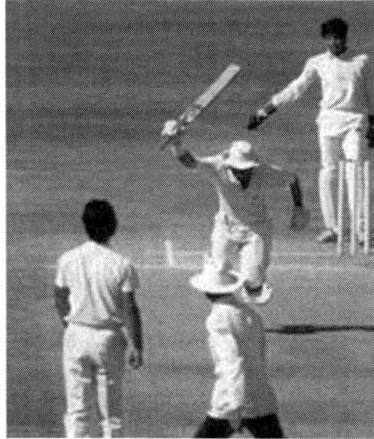

Sunil Gavaskar completing 10000 runs in Test cricket thus becoming the first one to do so

Like every other individual Gavaskar must be judged within the context of a broad perspective. At a time when India was not a cricket super-power, victories were few and far between. He had to play many different roles as a batter as he did not have the luxury of support that Bradman, Hammond, Richards and Sobers enjoyed. However, SMG was certainly more fortunate than George Headley and Hanif Mohammed – both fought single-handedly – for he had Gundappa Vishwanath in constant company.

As a product of Dadar Union in Matunga, he continued in the hallowed tradition of Mumbai cricket where every worthwhile batter was expected to play the long, grinding innings to tire down the opposition. He played the sheet anchor's role to perfection. Such was his control over situations and conditions that he would nurse the younger generations. He was the foundation – the Rock of Gavaskar – that never rocked no matter the gale, quake or eruption.

His reserved exterior was only a façade. Had no time for pretenders; still less for social climbers. His streak of radicalism unfortunately over-stepped its limits at times: 1975 World Cup; Lillee-Melbourne; Kingston and Calcutta crowds, among a few others. Thankfully the man realized his mistakes and regretted his impetuosity later. The will and the wish to admit one's mistake need courage. I am personally happy that my friend was able to rise above petty egoism and had the rare courage to admit his misdemeanours publicly. Very, very few can do so.

SMG's captaincy tenure too ran into heavy weather time and again. So engrossed was he with the end result that at times his methods came in for criticism. To him a cricket match was a *dharma-yudh*, to paraphrase Krishna at the Kurukshetra. Some of his tactics looked tactless. Once he declared the 1st innings of a Test match (admittedly, one day was washed out) at Eden around lunch on the 4th day! SMG put such a high premium on result that he would take to unnecessary means if the laws were on his side. At times he gave the distinct impression that he was not bothered about the niceties and the charms of the great game.

Yet the man has a sense of humour that is second to none. Extremely witty and knowledgeable, he is among the best speakers in the cricket community. His comments on paper or over-the-mike have earned universal admiration. He still remains the most sought-after commentator on television. His is the most respected voice in the world of cricket. No mean achievement that, for sure.

For the sake of his fellow cricketers, however, he rebelled and secured them the rights and the rewards that they deserved. He was a rebel in the best sense of the term. Like Bishen Bedi, Sunil Gavaskar became a rebel because of his high sense of self-respect and his love for his motherland. As a self-appointed spokesman for cricketers he became an unofficial cricket ombudsman.

His soul was his body; his body his soul. His thoughts and actions invariably coincided. He ruffled a lot of people as he went along whether as a cricketer, as a writer or as a commentator. Consequently, he evoked mixed reactions. Either one admired him; or hated him. No middle path as far as SMG was concerned. No one however could afford to ignore him, disregard him. His presence loomed large on the horizon of Indian cricket while he was playing as much as it is even now, 30 years after his retirement. Why is it that a person of such phenomenal achievement never received unstinted affection from all quarters? The chief reason could be that one who is infallible, invincible appears too big, too superior, too forbidding. They inspire awe, not affection. They stagger; they frighten. So, did Gavaskar. Sentiments, sensitivity, sensibility were not associated with him.

Yet with the help of his dear friend Jayanta Chatterji, he planned the emergence of The Sunil Gavaskar Foundation at Calcutta, where he invited Naresh Kumar, Vece Paes and me to become the Trustees. The Trust organized tours to UK and helped a whole generation of highly talented cricketers from all over India to find their feet in the world of cricket. He also involved in many social welfare projects but would not seek publicity for those.

SMG with the trustees of Sunil Gavaskar Foundation: music & sports aficionado Jayanta Chatterji and the author

Over the years his penmanship and his comments have evoked

the highest admiration from all quarters. His books are all best-sellers. His admirers are all over the world. He is actually the lord of all that he surveys. The man's attitude and approach as a cricket personality was and remains exemplary. His methods have over the years been magnificent on and off the field. He showed the world what the mind could do, what mental fitness meant. His confidence bordered on arrogance; his concentration imperturbable. His appetite for achievement was and still remains insatiable.

He brought dignity to Indians in the world of cricket. He gave us a shaded seat in the cricket sun. His Himalayan peaks of achievement made it easier for others who followed him to walk ten feet tall.

If Polly Umrigar be the chief architect of modern Indian cricket, then surely Bishen and Sunil would be the leading towers of the super-structure.

Printed in Great Britain
by Amazon